Rich Caterer's Bible

The Testament of Cuisine

TABLE OF CONTENTS

Page No.

The Revelation

A Few Introductory Thoughts   3
What This Book Contains   3
Should You or Shouldn't You?   5

The Book of Creative Beginnings
Creating Your Catering Identity

In the Beginning…   11
Choosing a Catering Style   12
Creating Your Catering Vision   13
Developing a Mission Statement   15
Constructing the Perfect Business Name   16
The *Wow* Factor: Creating the Ultimate
Feel-Good Experience   17

The Book of Heavenly Cuisine
Serving Fabulous Food

Cooking Like a Pro   23
The Rich Caterer's Menu   25
Making It Sizzle   30

The Book of Maximum Yields
Getting a Bigger Piece of the Pie

The Language of Numbers   41
A Measured Way to Riches   43
Conversions Are Crucial   46

Mind Your APs and EPs 48

Watch the Pennies and the Dollars Take
Care of Themselves 51

Un-Shrinking the Shrinkage 59

The Book of Calculated Riches
The Basics of Costing and Pricing

Food Costing 101: Ingredient Costing
for Rich Caterers 65

Food Costing 202: Recipe Costing for
Rich Caterers 82

Pricing for Value 92

The Book of Profitable Portions
Cleverly Controlling Food Quantities

Size Does Matter 99

Smaller Pieces = Bigger Profits 100

Cash in the Trash 102

Counting Is Critical 107

The Book of Savvy Purchasing
How to Get More for Less

Pretend It's Your New Car 113

Ordering Food Intelligently 114

Buying in Bulk 133

Flexibility and the Bottom Line 133

The Book of Superabundance
Part 1: The Leftover Challenge

The Client vs. the Caterer 141

Guaranteed Money 142

The Generous Fool 144

Part 2: Dealing Effectively With Leftovers

Developing Detailed Policies 149

Putting Food Back in the Loop 150

Safe Food Handling Is the Key 152

Creatively Transforming Leftover Food 156

In Conclusion 159

Appendices

Appendix 1 - Yield Percentages of Common Fruits and Vegetables 161

Appendix 2 - Sample Menus 165

THE REVELATION

A Few Introductory Thoughts

The demand for good quality catering has increased tremendously over the years. With this demand, the need for experienced caterers has gone up as well. The number of people who become professional caterers is increasing daily and with good reason. Many caterers enjoy profits that are the highest in the food service industry.

According to Packaged Facts' *Catering Trends in U.S. Foodservice*, the estimate of catering sales for 2011 was approximately $15.5 billion with an increase in 2012 to almost $16.5 billion. Energetic people like you see those crazy numbers and dream about what it would be like to have your own profitable catering business.

As an owner myself, I can attest to the fact that running a catering business can be both financially rewarding and enjoyable. Whether you cater events on a full-time or part-time basis, the opportunities are excellent, and there's a high potential for expansion and growth.

You don't need to have a business degree from an Ivy League school to become a successful caterer. Operating a catering business, large or small, can be achieved by anyone with average intelligence. However, the income potential of any catering business depends greatly on excellent money management and organizational skills. The ability to keep operating costs down while maintaining high quality food and service is essential.

What This Book Contains

Will you learn all there is to know about being a caterer in this book? No, a book that contained *everything* that someone needs to know about catering (if there could even be such a thing) would be enormous. It would take a long time to read and would quickly become out-of-date. That's because the catering industry is always changing. This year's trends could be next year's old news. Fortunately for you, almost all of the information that you need to know about catering is available in various books and on the Internet. Experts in many areas including real estate, marketing, sanitation regulations, legal issues, etc. have written numerous articles and books on those subjects. I suggest that you take the time to research those as well.

Is this a cookbook? No. In fact, the first thing you might notice about this publication is that it doesn't contain any real recipes. Many books that deal with catering fill almost half of their pages with seemingly unimportant fluff, such as "the perfect way to prepare meatloaf," or "grandma's secret recipe for banana bread." While this is nice information, it does almost nothing to help you run a well-managed and profitable business.

The *Rich Caterer's Bible* is a collection of books that contains a two-part *revelation* of what we consider to be the *most important* money-making ideas, business forms, and activities you need to become a successful caterer. In addition, we're going to reveal many wealth-creating secrets and insider information that other authors either don't know about or wouldn't touch with a ten-foot pole!

This first part, "The Testament of Cuisine," focuses on many aspects of the food production sector of professional catering. These include quality food preparation, accurate costing and pricing, proper food portioning, savvy purchasing, creativity in transforming leftovers, and more.

This volume is serious about increasing the profits of your current or future catering business through intelligence and self-development. In addition, this book contains a thorough discussion of the many skills and techniques necessary for catering success. Don't jump off a bridge if you're lacking in any of these areas. Each skill can be studied and nurtured until it's mastered. Some skills will take longer to master than others. Luckily, you probably already possess some of the skills included here and can check them off the list.

For instance, you may have a real knack for interior design that you learned while working at a retail store. This will come in handy as a caterer. Perhaps you've been cooking since the age of twelve, when mom broke her arm and, well, *somebody* had to do it! The cooking knowledge you gained will be valuable indeed. Have you worked as an employee trainer, an accountant, a waitress, a sign painter, a supervisor, or bartender? All of these experiences will fit on your caterer's resume. The fact is, catering is not rocket science and almost *any* experience that you've had in your life will help you. Some experiences are better than others, and I'll pinpoint those crucial areas as we move along the road to catering riches.

One other piece of good news is that you can start out with a very small, low pressure catering business and learn many of these important skills as you go along. You can practice until you make it perfect. Let's say that you want to start out slow and just sell homemade birthday cakes to your clients. Perhaps your math skills aren't the greatest. However, you'd still like have some clue as to whether your business is making a profit or not. Start with some simple costing procedures (shown in "The Book of Calculated Riches"). Then, take your time and practice, practice, practice until your costing and pricing skills become second nature to you. Soon after, you might be making weekly deposits into your catering bank account.

Before we get started on the meat and potatoes of this book (pun intended), there's one last thing I'd like you to know. Being a professional caterer, while fun and exciting, may not be a good fit for you personally. The rest of this chapter will help you decide if you're the type of individual who has what it takes to become a rich caterer. Read carefully, consider all of the pros and cons and then make your choice.

Should You or Shouldn't You?

So you say that you want to become a rich caterer? Well then, maybe I should tell you upfront that running a successful catering business is demanding and not for the faint of heart. Many people start a catering business only to find out that it doesn't fit with their desired lifestyle or family responsibilities. Most people who've made a career in the catering business enjoy their work, and that's why they continue to do it. But, if you're lazy or want other people to do the work for you, your business will ultimately fail. The most successful caterers work alongside their employees and keep a personal eye on the bottom line.

Before you hop headfirst into the catering abyss, it's a good idea to stop right here and do a little soul searching. Take a few moments now to consider what this mysterious journey to the promised land of catering will require from you.

I suggest you start by constructing a list of the positive and negative aspects of owning a catering business. If you haven't thought about them before, this would be the time to do it. The owner of a catering business has many of the same advantages and disadvantages that owners of all businesses have. While the advantages are always available, the disadvantages, for the most part, can be overcome. So, here for your painstaking consideration, are the pros and cons of becoming a professional caterer.

General advantages include:

- Many extra tax deductions are available to you.
- You're challenged every day.
- You work because you want to, not because the boss asked you to do it.
- *You* determine how things get done and where you work.
- You experience the excitement and thrill of carving out your own destiny.
- You can earn significantly more than what a salaried employee earns.
- Having your own business frees you up to live the lifestyle you want.
- You'll help make the world a better place with your products or services.
- You'll be able to work in an area of expertise that you really enjoy.

General disadvantages include:

- You always need to be at the top of your game (when you're the boss, it's easy to procrastinate).
- You may have to take a large financial risk.
- You may end up spending a lot of time attending to the details of running your business.
- You may find that your income is not steady.
- You may have to deal with some unpleasantness, such as firing an employee or refusing to hire a friend or relative.

- You may have to learn many new disciplines, such as bookkeeping, inventory control, production planning, employee scheduling, advertising and promotion, market research, and other general management tasks.

In addition to those listed above, there are also advantages and disadvantages specific to a catering business. These include:

Specific Advantages:

- You usually work with many young, energetic people.
- You can forecast sales and expenditures well ahead of time.
- You can schedule your free time based on a specific work schedule.
- Advance deposits mean you have most of your money before the event.
- Your inventory and costs are primarily limited to the number of events you schedule.
- You can be selective about who you do business with.
- Catered events can be a huge thrill to execute.
- You can get a real sense of satisfaction from your work.

Specific Disadvantages:

- Sanitation problems can close your business.
- Scrutiny of your food and service is intense.
- Theft of food or alcohol can be a problem.
- Most of your inventory is perishable and must be used quickly.
- The majority of your business is done on the weekends.
- Stress can become extreme on the day of an event.
- Work areas can be dangerous (food slicers, knives, fire, excess water, etc.).
- Work can be difficult (heavy lifting, excessive heat, crowded work areas, etc.).

If you're thinking of starting out small, here are some other things to consider.

General Pros and Cons of Starting a Smaller Home-Based Business Include:

- Pro: Your operating costs will be lower than if you're renting space and paying utilities.
- Con: You may run out of space at home when your business starts growing.
- Pro: Your commute will be shorter.
- Con: You're more vulnerable to interruptions from family, neighbors, and others.
- Pro: Your start-up costs will be lower.
- Con: You may be less accessible to suppliers.
- Pro: Your business can be conducted outside normal weekday business hours.

There are, of course, more pros and cons to opening a catering business than can be mentioned here. However, I think these examples are sufficient to help you make your final decision.

Okay, it's time to make up your mind. Are you going to put on your swimsuit and take a plunge into the catering pool, or are you going to sit on your lounge chair and drink a margarita? I'll give you a full thirty seconds to think it over, starting...*now* (insert Final Jeopardy music here). Well, what have you decided? Pick one of the following responses and follow the instructions.

"No Deal" Well done! You are a very self-aware person who knows his or her limitations. The fact that you said no at this time means that you probably don't really have the desire to make this catering thing work anyway. You've just saved yourself a lot of sleepless nights while your business fails miserably. Close the book at this point and give it to one of your more adventurous friends.

"I'll Do It!" Outstanding! You are also a very self-aware person who knows his or her limitations. The difference is you're willing to transcend those current limitations and turn them into strengths. I congratulate you on your courage and positive attitude. These traits will be extremely useful on your way to becoming a rich caterer. Continue reading; it's time to talk about creating your exciting new business.

THE BOOK OF
CREATIVE BEGINNINGS
Creating Your Catering Identity

In the Beginning...

When you first start out, before you even think of doing anything else, I suggest that you examine the community where you're planning to do business. You must find out the likes and dislikes of the people you hope to serve. Armed with this information, you'll be able to make intelligent choices about the identity, vision, and direction of your brand-new catering business.

There are a couple of ways to evaluate your market. Some people go to city hall and research potential customers based on demographic information. Relevant information might include:

- Population breakdown by age
- Forecast of population growth for the next five to ten years
- Number of households
- Number of two-income households
- Average family income
- Average family size
- Average education level

After you're done acquiring the data, you'll have to sift through the pile and try to determine what it all means. For me, this method leaves too much up to your own interpretation, and the conclusions you draw might not be valid.

The second, and I feel that the best, way to evaluate your market is the one we used when opening our business. My partner and I found out about our potential clients by going to our future competition. You might be saying, "Are you kidding? Your future competition! How does that work?"

Well, it's a simple process that doesn't take very much time at all. First of all, get a sample menu or catering packet from every caterer in your area. Ask your friends to help you. The more information you can get, the better it'll be. Gathering this information will allow you to find out how your potential clients are *already* spending their money on catered events. You'll find out popular styles of food, the price range for each style, extra items that are offered for sale, the range of service charges, sample contracts, and much more. Do you see more on-premise or off-premise catering? (If you don't understand the difference, don't worry, it will be explained shortly.) While you're at the other caterers, you (or your friends) can ask questions of the manager or event planner. Ask questions such as:

- What type of service style is most popular? Is it sit-down, buffet, or family style?
- Do they offer services like delivery, drive-through, or takeout?
- Do they partner with florists, photographers, bakeries, etc.?
- Do they have a list of satisfied clients that you can call for information about their completed events?

By going to your competition for answers, you'll find a treasure chest full of information to help you start your business.

Choosing a Catering Style

Now that you have some information about your community's preferences, it's time to determine what type of catering business you want to open. Let's start with choosing from the different categories of catering. Select one or more of the categories below.

On-Premise Catering: On-premise catering is catering for any event that's held on the physical premises of the establishment or facility that is producing the function. In other words, you serve the event at *your* place. This is the simplest type of full-service catering. You cook the food in *your* kitchen and serve the food in *your* dining room.

Off-Premise Catering: Off-premise catering is catering for any event that takes place in a remote location. This could include a client's home, a park, an art gallery, or even a parking lot. In other words, you serve the event at *their* place. It means that the staff, food, and decor must all be transported to that location. Off-premise catering often involves producing food at a central kitchen and then delivering it to the event location. Sometimes, part or all of the food production is carried out at the event site.

At times, off-premise caterers must depend on generators for electricity. They might also need to rely on deliveries of potable water, devise their own trash collection system and otherwise rough it. Obviously, you need to have dependable vehicles and a strong stomach for this type of catering. Many things can go wrong in a hurry. My suggestion is, if you want to attempt off-premise catering, start very small—perhaps parties for fewer than fifty people. That'll give you a chance to get the hang of it before you commit yourself too fully.

Takeout Catering: Takeout catering is very simple. You make the food and put it on, or in, disposable containers. The client orders their food ahead of time, shows up at the agreed upon time, pays you your money, and takes the food home. Bada bing, bada boom. On the surface, this seems like a no-brainer. However, any time that you allow someone else to reheat and serve your food, there's the potential for sanitation problems. Questions to ask yourself are:

- Will the customer reheat the food to the proper temperature?
- Will the customer cool the leftover food quickly in order to minimize bacterial growth?
- Will the customer sneeze or cough on the food before serving it to guests?

Just thinking about the possibilities could drive you crazy! My suggestion for takeout catering is to clearly mark all of the items to be heated with your own reheating instructions. In addition, give clients a small card with general cooling instructions for all hot food. At least this way you can cover yourself a little bit and let the client know that sanitation is important to your business.

Creating Your Catering Vision

Once you've chosen the category of catering that you want to be involved in, it's time to give your new business some *personality*. Of course you want your business to serve food that's delicious and offer great customer service. Every caterer wants to do that, but they all do it in a different way. How are you going to separate yourself from those other caterers? What's your vision? What will you offer that makes your catering service unique? Your answers to these questions will depend on what you've learned from your market evaluation and your own special skill set. For instance, when we looked at the information from caterers in our community, we concluded the following:

- Many people wanted simple, good quality food and basic service with no frills.
- A smaller, but *significant* percentage of people wanted upscale catering with fancier food items and more attentive service.
- There was a definite lack of upscale catering in the community.
- The few upscale caterers in the area were extremely busy and successful.
- Most caterers in the community were very limited in their menu selections and service style.
- The prices on the current caterers' menus were generally lower because of their location (rural).

My partner and I brought our own set of skills to the business. I am well trained in culinary arts, and my partner has a strong service background, as she had worked as a server and restaurant owner for many years. We were sure that our qualifications would enable us to offer something that other caterers couldn't... *flexibility.*

We wrote a menu that contained both simple and upscale items. That allowed us to satisfy clients who wanted good food at an economical price while providing the variety of items necessary to satisfy a choosier clientele. We were also able to offer a range of table service options—including simple buffet, plated service, and family style. We decided that our catering business was going to offer the best customer service in the area, no matter which menu they chose. Our clients were not going to get less service just because they spent less money. Once we came up with our business concept, our direction was clear.

Developing a Mission Statement

When you reach this point of clarity, you may want to think about creating a mission statement. The mission statement for your business will define the main purpose of your organization—the reason for its existence. If ever you feel that you've lost your way, your mission statement should bring you back to what's most important. No business is required to have a mission statement, and many businesses get along just fine without one. However, a well-written mission statement conveys a commitment to your employees and clients. It gives you and your catering business an *identity*. A mission statement should require little or no explanation, and its length is less important than its power. For example, one of Nike's now famous mission statements was: "CRUSH REEBOK." It requires no explanation, their objective was unmistakable, and it motivated everyone associated with Nike. Instead, Nike could have stated their mission as, "to be the best shoe company with the best customer service," but that would have done little to inspire the troops. Don't make that mistake with your own mission statement—make it passionate and inspiring, not bland and boring. Now, your mission statement probably won't be as aggressive as Nike's, but I think you get the idea. Consider some other famous examples:

- PEPSI: "Beat Coke."
- 3M: "To solve unsolved problems innovatively."
- Mary Kay Cosmetics: "To give unlimited opportunity to women."
- Wal-Mart: "To give ordinary folk the chance to buy the same thing as rich people."
- Walt Disney: "To make people happy."

That last one is my favorite. If you've ever gone to a Disney theme park, you know that they bend over backward to make sure that you have an enjoyable experience. You could think a long time and never come up with a better mission statement. You can borrow it if you like, and I'm sure that Walt Disney would have been thrilled.

Constructing the Perfect Business Name

Choosing a name for your business is one of the most exciting choices you'll get to make. Start by using your mission statement as a guide. This will allow you to choose a name that fits the direction of your business and states what you're trying to accomplish. Think about what's going to set you apart from other caterers, and showcase that with your name. If possible, come up with a name that connects with the people in your community, something that they can all understand and identify with. Be as creative as you want to be; people expect caterers to be creative. Here are a few strategies for crafting a business name:

Research: You certainly don't want a name that someone else already has, so start with the phone book and look at the names of all the caterers in your area. Most of them are pretty boring, so you wouldn't want to use those anyway. Write down the names that you think are good and set those aside for later comparison. Once you've done that, you're ready for the next step.

Experiment: Write down a list of descriptive words that sound really attractive to you, such as extraordinary, distinctive, elite, exceptional, amazing, and so on. Next write down words related to food or cooking. These might include: fare, cuisine, meal, etc. Finally, construct another list of words associated with service, such as: satisfy, please, delight, thrill, and entertain. Once you have created these lists, start mixing them together to see if you can identify a phrase that pleases you, like "Distinctive Delights" or "Amazing Meals." That's all there is to it. When you hit on one that strikes your fancy, you'll find your new business name. If you're well known in your community, naming your business after yourself might also help to draw in clients. If I were choosing another name, for example, I might choose, "Jeff's Amazing Meals" or "Distinctive Delights by Jeff."

Choose a name that everyone can pronounce: I know that this sounds obvious, but you'd be surprised at the names people come up with. Don't use foreign words either, such as "Le Pain Du Jour Catering" (bread of the day catering), because if people can't say the name, they're not going to call you. Stick with English and keep it short.

Alphabetical Order: Some caterers think that if they put their name at the beginning of the listings in the yellow pages, potential clients will see their listing first and it will generate business. First of all, anyone who chooses a caterer because their listing says, "AAA Catering Service" must not be very picky. Personally, I don't know if I want to be serving clients who don't even care who their caterer is. Secondly, you'll never attract a client who's looking for a more upscale (and thus more lucrative) experience with a generic name like that. If you want to be in the front of the listings, choose a descriptive word that starts with "A" for your business name, like "Amazing Meals." That way, you can have the best of both worlds.

The Wow Factor: Creating the Ultimate Feel-Good Experience

Have you ever attended a large, catered event that blew you away? Literally, as soon as you walked in the door, something—the decorations, the food, or the service—energized you. Maybe your eyes bugged out of your head or your jaw dropped an inch or two. This happens to foodies like us whenever we experience a presentation that's particularly well done. When we find ourselves in these situations, there's usually just one word that comes to mind—*wow*!

The last part of creating your catering identity involves adopting a way of doing business that consistently provides that *wow* factor. You'll promise your clients a great experience and then deliver something even better. It takes a special person to commit to this type of catering business, and it'll make you look like a diamond when most other caterers are rhinestones. You'll shine brighter, because very few caterers feel the need to go the extra mile the way you do.

But maybe you're skeptical, and I can understand that, because creating a wow factor sounds like a lot of extra time and money. You're correct in that assumption; it certainly will take more effort and a few extra dollars per event, but some good things will happen to your business because of it. Let's examine a few:

Minimal Marketing Expense: Once you're recognized as a wow-factor caterer, you'll never need to spend a dime to market your business for the rest of your life. Never? That's right, *never!* While you may need to spend a little money to get your name out there initially, you won't need to do it again once you're business is firmly established. Oh, you might *want* to spend some of your riches on advertising so that your business expands much faster, but even without the extra boost, it will expand.

How can I make such an absurd claim? Think of it this way. One happy customer tells about ten people about their positive experience. Most of us have heard that statistic before and understand the power of good word-of-mouth advertising. But because you're a wow-factor caterer, and you make a habit of exceeding expectations, your clients are going to have an even *more* memorable experience. They'll be absolutely chomping at the bit to tell someone about the incredible food and service that you've provided for them. Do you know how many people a gleeful client talks to about their wonderful experience? They tell *everyone*! Plus, it's not just the clients who'll be talking. The guests who attended the event will praise your business to their friends, too. That's not just *good* advertising, that's *incredible* word-of-mouth advertising. As long as your clients continue to have those super-positive experiences, they'll continue to market your catering business for you and develop into return customers as well!

Employee Recognition: Almost all of us have been employees at some point in our lives. Working for someone else can be difficult, and I think you'll agree that recognizing employees for a job well done is very important. Many times, we're so busy during the heat of battle that we don't think about giving our employees a kind word until much later or even the next day. But that's not a problem when you're a wow-factor caterer who involves your staff in exceeding the clients' expectations. As your employees are working, guests will be coming up to them on a regular basis to tell them how great they are and what a wonderful job they've done. Complete strangers will walk up to your staff, shake their hands, and tell them that everything they did that day was just fabulous. Believe me; your employees will love the extra recognition. Better yet, they'll enjoy working for you because it's a fun, feel-good environment. Ultimately, this builds long-term employee loyalty and saves the time and money involved in training new staff.

Creating Memories: One of the best results of being a wow-factor caterer is your ability, as an individual and as a business, to directly and positively influence your clients' lives. We talk a lot about making money in this book, and that is extremely important for your future. However, you'll also be fortunate enough to be intimately involved in something that may be considered priceless. I'm talking about creating positive memories for your clients, their families, and their guests. Hopefully, you and your staff will provide food and service to people in the midst of the happiest days of their *entire lives!* Your ability to exceed client expectations will help to insure that happiness and create good memories that will last a lifetime. You'll know that you've created a memory when you see someone enter the beautifully decorated hall and start to cry, or laugh giddily, or excitedly exclaim, (you can say it with me), "*Wow!*"

So, what do you say? Have I persuaded you to build your business on exceeding customer expectations by becoming a wow-factor caterer? I hope so, because if you truly want to aspire to the title of rich caterer...

> **Exceeding expectations is the first *nonnegotiable*, *absolutely essential* part of running a catering business that attracts big money.**

What does it take to continually exceed expectations and become a wow-factor caterer?

It takes a burning desire to always provide the best food and service possible. You must adopt a habit of giving more than is expected, and do it with a flourish that impresses your clients and their guests. Be unwavering in your belief that giving the customer more than they expect is the only way to generate big profits. "Just good enough to get by" will never, ever be good enough for you.

I'm not saying anything new here either, because most caterers understand the link between outstanding food and service and high profits. But it's one thing to know this and quite another to follow through and execute it for every single event. I've been to quite a few events where the food or service just wasn't up to par, and I'm sure you have, too. It's an easy trap to fall into, especially for established caterers. Don't let it happen to you. Your desire to present your best effort must never waver, because presenting just average food or service will never separate you from the rest of the catering pack or make you rich.

One more thing that's essential for creating the wow factor is to preach the benefits of exceptional food and service to your employees. Train your staff to believe in your mission as much as you do. You can be as dedicated to exceeding expectations as anyone in the history of catering, but if your staff doesn't believe in it, you're toast. There's no way that you can do it all by yourself. Take the time to train your employees well. Make sure that they understand your company's mission and are committed to it. Your personal wealth depends on it.

THE BOOK OF HEAVENLY CUISINE
Serving Fabulous Food

Cooking Like a Pro

Serving fabulous food is the second *nonnegotiable*, *absolutely essential* part of running a catering business that attracts big money.

Are you a whiz in the kitchen? If you are, that's fantastic! You're one step closer to becoming a wealthy caterer. If you're not, we need to get real for a moment. As a caterer, you'll be serving food to hundreds of people at every event. Do you really think that your business will generate large profits if you don't know very much about food or cooking? That's like saying the owner of a computer store is going to make a fortune without knowing anything about computers. It just doesn't make any sense. There's some hope for you, though. There aren't too many basic principles or procedures in the culinary arts that are difficult to master. You might have some trouble with ice carvings, delicate vegetable garnishes, or other decorative pieces—that's to be expected. However, most cooking procedures are simple and just take a little patience and practice. That being said, home cooking skills are *not* the same as commercial cooking skills. So many other factors enter into food preparation besides shopping, slicing, and heating. There's a huge difference between doing a dinner party for twelve people and serving five hundred guests at a wedding. Let's compare the two:

	Dinner for twelve	Wedding for five hundred
Preparation time	one day	up to one week
Refrigeration/ freezers	one standard refrigerator/freezer combo	two commercial refrigerators and one commercial freezer
Pots, pans, and utensils	two or three loads in the dishwasher	around two hundred loads in a commercial dish machine
Trash	one large trash bag	about a dozen large trash bags
Service time	one to two hours	thirty to forty minutes

	Dinner for twelve	Wedding for five hundred
Clean-up time	one to two hours	six to eight hours
Environment	semi-stressful party atmosphere	extreme stress that may induce heart palpitations

That gives you an idea of the basics. As you can see, food preparation for a large function is a very involved, time-consuming process. That's why people need professional caterers to do it for them. The degree to which you're skilled in culinary arts can be your saving grace or your deadly downfall. It really pays to know what you're doing in the kitchen. Let me give you a few suggestions:

- If you have low to average cooking skills, take some classes at the local cooking school or community college. You'll practice your basic skills and get to learn the lingo. Then, if you choose not to become a caterer, you can still give a fantastic dinner party.
- If you have average to above-average cooking skills, I suggest that you get some experience in a real catering business. Call one of the local caterers and volunteer to do some food preparation work for their next event. Most likely, they'll take you on as long as you do good work and stay out of the way. While you're staying out of the way, you'll be making mental notes of everything you see, so that you can write it down later. If you do well the first time, they may call you back again for their next event, and this time they may even *pay* you. The more involved you get with the people that work there, the more knowledge you'll have. When you advance enough to prepare food along with the professionals, you'll be well on your way to opening your own profitable business.
- If you haven't already, make sure that you become familiar with a variety of professional cooking books. I'm not talking about books written for the home cook like *The Joy of Cooking* or *The Betty Crocker Cookbook.* I mean professional cooking textbooks that include the basic knowledge of classical cuisine, complete with standardized recipes, procedures, and photos. If you like

to cook (and you should), these are fascinating books that are really fun to read and will open up the world of commercial cooking to any novice. When you've become really good at basic food preparation, these textbooks will serve as part of your business's reference library. You can find books that deal with professional cooking at any good bookstore or online.

- No matter what level of culinary skills you have, practice as often as possible to become familiar with all of the basic preparations and procedures. That way, you can prepare most of the menu items yourself to save labor costs. Even if you hire a chef, you'll still need to have some basic cooking knowledge and skills in case of an emergency. You should be able to jump into the kitchen and help at a moment's notice.

To sum it up, having good basic food preparation skills is crucial to the success of your business. If you need to learn more about food and cooking, don't be stressed about it. Cooking food is supposed to be *fun*. It can be a marvelous adventure, because there are new things to learn all the time. I've been cooking professionally for almost forty years, and I still enjoy it. So dig in, get dirty, and by all means, play with your food.

The Rich Caterer's Menu

A thoughtfully developed menu that includes customer preferences, flexibility, and fair pricing will generate the cash flow necessary to support other areas of your business, such as service and decor. Until you develop a satisfactory menu, your business will not prosper as it should.

The first thing that I suggest you do is create a menu development file. Be sure to include food preferences of your local area. Your initial research should involve examining the catering menus that you obtained from your competitors in the previous chapter. Gather the menus together and look them over carefully to recognize patterns. Keep your eyes peeled for general and specific food items that clients in your area might prefer. If specific items such as prime rib or baked chicken keep on popping up, write them down. You can be pretty sure that if an item is mentioned on numerous menus, it must be a favorite.

Next, it's a good idea to talk to family, friends, and other well-known people in the community. Ask them what their favorite food was when they were growing up, and why. Talk about foods that they really like but nobody makes anymore. Inquire about the types of comfort food they enjoy and how they like it prepared. You can learn a lot about local likes and dislikes simply by talking to people about food. It's a favorite subject for most people, and sometimes they really enjoy the conversation. You may find it hard to get them to *stop* talking! When you're done interviewing, add the information you receive to your menu development file.

When you have a thorough record of community food preferences and family favorites, look over the list carefully and decide which items you're definitely going to put on your menu. Delete any items that you may not have the skills to make, or will be difficult to prepare for large groups (you can always take special requests at a later time if necessary).

Now we're going to spark it up a little with some specials. Do you have any dishes that you make exceptionally well and would be proud to serve? This could be something that your family particularly enjoys, or something wild you dreamed up in the dorm kitchen that everyone raved about. These dishes could be risky, but if your college friends really liked it, I'll bet a lot of other people will too. The worst that could happen is that it doesn't sell and you take it off of the menu next time. Putting specialty items on your catering menu is like putting your signature on it. In addition, it offers something different that no other caterer in the community has. Best of all, your clients will feel that they're getting something special when they order it for their event.

After putting the information together, you should have a list of menu items that correspond well with your community's preferences and your own talents. The next step is to divide your menu into categories.

Buffet/plated service menu:

A good portion of any caterer's menu is devoted to buffet and sit-down (plated) service for large groups. This category includes weddings, birthdays, anniversaries, etc. Usually, any food that can be put on a buffet line can also be plated and served to the guests at their tables, so that's why they're grouped together. Now you have to make a decision. What types of food are you going to offer, and in what price ranges? You don't need to know the prices yet, but you do need to separate your menu items into low, medium, and higher priced options. In our business, we describe our menu options as traditional, premium, and elegant. Let me explain how it works.

When clients come to talk to us about booking an event, we ask them what type of service they would like. Usually it's a buffet. Then we hand them one of our menus and guide them to the section on buffets. In this section, they'll find three categories of menu items:

Traditional menu: Items that are easy to make and use less costly ingredients. This menu is the least expensive of our offerings.

Premium menu: Items that are a bit more difficult to prepare and/or use slightly more expensive ingredients. This menu will be a little more expensive for the client.

Elegant menu: Items that are the most time consuming to prepare and/or use very expensive ingredients. This is the highest priced menu that we offer.

When setting up your menu, use a simple table and separate the pricing categories. Just to be different, let's say that your categories are identified as: homestyle (least expensive), select (more expensive), and gourmet (most expensive). Using those choices, your table should look like this:

HOMESTYLE	SELECT	GOURMET

Next, we'll pick a general menu category and select items that fit into it. I like to start with the main entrees, so let's begin with a meat item such as beef. First, identify the section you're working on by adding beef to the left-hand column. Then you can start adding the menu items that belong in the beef section. A homestyle beef menu item might be Sliced Roast Beef, a select item would be Italian Roast Beef, and a gourmet item would be Roast Prime Rib au Jus. That's an example of three very similar menu items that you can separate into categories based upon difficulty of preparation and/or cost. Continuing with the same procedure, let's add Salisbury Steak, Swiss Steak, and Grilled NY Strip Steak. On the next line, follow those choices with Beef Stew, Hungarian Goulash, and Beef Bourguignon. When everything is done, the table should look like this:

	HOMESTYLE	SELECT	GOURMET
BEEF	Sliced Roast Beef	Italian Roast Beef	Roast Prime Rib au Jus
	Salisbury Steak	Swiss Steak	Grilled NY Strip Steak
	Beef Stew	Hungarian Goulash	Beef Bourguignon

You'll then divide the rest of your beef menu items into categories in the same way. After you finish with the beef selections, you'll continue with poultry, pork, seafood, and so on. This will give your clients a good selection of items in each category. The table should look similar to this one:

	HOMESTYLE	SELECT	GOURMET
BEEF	Sliced Roast Beef	Italian Roast Beef	Roast Prime Rib au Jus
	Salisbury Steak	Swiss Steak	Grilled NY Strip Steak
	Beef Stew	Hungarian Goulash	Beef Bourguignonne
PORK	Sliced Roast Pork	BBQ Pork Roast	Stuffed Roast Pork Loin
	Pan-Fried Pork Cutlets	Pork Chops with Mushroom Gravy	Smoked Pork Chops
	Ham Loaf	Smoked Pork Shoulder	Spiral Sliced Ham
POULTRY	Baked Chicken	Baked Lemon Pepper Chicken	Herb Crusted Baked Chicken
	Chicken ala King	Chicken Divan	Chicken with Wine and Mushrooms
	Grilled Chicken Breast	Herbed/Lemon Chicken Breast	Chicken Breast Cacciatore

SEAFOOD	Baked Fish with Butter	Baked Cod with Lemon Pepper	Baked Salmon with Dill Sauce
	Crab Newburg	Crab Cakes	Steamed Crab Legs with Lemon Butter
	Shrimp Jambalaya	Shrimp Scampi	Peel and Eat Shrimp

You'll have many more items in number than the few written here. There's no need to have the same amount of items in each category, either. Develop this table to be a reflection of the eating styles within your community. Maybe there's a large percentage of vegetarians in your area. If so, you'll need to include good vegetarian choices in the table.

When all of the items you've chosen are divided into categories, it's time to add a little wow factor to your menu. People who see our menu for the first time are usually shocked at the sheer size of it. Most caterers in our area give customers a menu that consists of, at most, three or four pages. When a client receives one of our menus, do you know what they get? A nicely bound, twenty-six-page *booklet* printed on quality paper that offers a seemingly endless variety of food choices for their upcoming event. Of course, you know what customers say when they look at it—*"Wow!"*

What do you think happens when prospective clients take our menu home and compare it to the other puny, unimaginative menus that they've collected? They see that our business has a real commitment to excellence and a desire to exceed their expectations. After the initial shock wears off, customers are genuinely excited about looking through our menu and making their choices. They'll show the menu to their family and friends, who also get excited about it. Remember, you only have one chance to make a first impression, so make your menu a wow experience for the customer.

How do you put all of that incredible variety into your menu? The first thing I suggest you do is look at the initial items on your menu and then think of similar recipes that you could prepare with little or no extra effort or ingredients. For instance, you already offer Sliced Roast Pork, so let's expand the menu with more roasted items. You could include Italian Roast Pork, BBQ Roast Pork Loin, Roast Pork Tenderloins, Sliced Baked Ham, and so forth. In the poultry section, you could add Baked Italian Chicken, Roast Duck, Sliced Roast Turkey, Roast Cornish Hen, etc.

When the entrée section is finished, you can move on to the vegetable side dishes. Use the same style of chart, including homestyle, select, and gourmet categories. Let's say that you want to include Seasoned Green Beans as a lower-cost vegetable side dish on your menu. Without much extra effort, you could add Green Beans Almandine, Green Beans with Mushrooms, Green Beans Au Gratin, Green Beans with Bacon and Onions, Green Bean Casserole, and so on. The lower cost Seasoned Broccoli could be made into Seasoned Broccoli and Cauliflower, Broccoli Almandine, Broccoli Au Gratin, Deep Fried Broccoli, and so forth. Decide what price column all of these selections would fit into and move ahead to other vegetables, such as corn, carrots, peas, etc.

Are you starting to get the picture? Use that process for your entire menu. Take something that's simple and make it better without a lot of extra expense or effort. Before you know it, you'll have hundreds of items that shouldn't be very difficult to make but that will add real variety. Feel free to look at our sample menus in the appendix at the back of this volume for inspiration and assistance.

Offering a large number of menu choices to your customers can be a scary thing, because more will be expected from the food production staff regarding their knowledge and expertise. But that's where your solid grasp of basic cooking principles comes into play. Your knowledge and experience in cooking will allow you to handle almost any menu item, even if it takes a little extra practice. When you're able to prepare each item on the menu, train your staff to do them just as well as you.

Making It Sizzle

Remember, serving fabulous food is the second nonnegotiable, absolutely essential part of running a catering business that attracts big money. As important as it is to give your clients a professional menu with lots of choices, if the food isn't prepared perfectly, you'll just be another average caterer.

That's why the food you serve to your customers must *dazzle* them at every event. The quality of your food must be consistently high, no matter what it takes. Again, this is where your knowledge and culinary skills will come to the rescue. When you think about it, it doesn't take much more effort to prepare a high quality food product than it does a shabby one. For me, the thought of my guests really enjoying my food was incentive enough to do an exceptional job. Here are a few simple rules that I've used over the years that have helped me to exceed my clients' expectations.

- Rule #1: Always use natural stocks and broths in your cooking.

  Stocks are made by simmering leftover bones (usually chicken) with flavorful vegetables. Making fresh stock doesn't require a lot of skill; it just cooks for a long time. If you schedule stock-making as a regular part of your kitchen's food production, the process becomes easier.
  Broths are simply the cooking liquid that's left over after simmering raw meat. Chicken broth is the most versatile and available. Best of all, if you already simmer chicken for casseroles, soup, or salads, the broth is *free*!
  The difference in flavor between natural stocks and commercial bases is enormous. While there are some acceptable premade sauce or gravy mixes on the market, only use them when you're in a pinch. If you're forced to use the mixes because of time or cost issues, use natural stock or broth in the mix instead of water to enhance the flavor.
  In addition to natural stocks and broths, add the flavorful drippings from your roasting pans to soups, sauces, and gravies for an even more superior product.

- Rule #2: Almost always make your food from scratch.

  If you're not making 90 percent of your food from scratch, why the heck did you take all of that time to study cooking? Your clients expect a fabulous, professionally cooked meal, and it's up to you to deliver it. The caterers who make the most money are the ones who truly care about serving wonderful food.
  I'm not saying that you need to serve Beef Medallions with Truffle Sauce or Pheasant Under Glass to make an impression on your customers. That would be missing the point. What I *am* telling you is that you can't impress your guests with the quality of your food unless you make most of it from scratch.

Does that mean that you should never use any convenience foods or partially prepared products? It doesn't mean that at all. We occasionally use convenience foods in our business, but we always try to make them better and more appealing.

For instance, if you're going to serve baked beans at a picnic, don't just open up a can of baked beans, heat them up, and call it done. I'm sure that you've seen this before and can agree that the beans are runny, somewhat tasteless, and *not* very impressive. I'd be embarrassed to serve something like that! What you need to do is add a little wow factor to get people talking.

We've served baked beans at many functions and always use the canned ones as a foundation. Before we served them, however, we cooked them briefly with ketchup, brown sugar, onions, mustard, and bacon. After cooling, the beans were allowed to rest in the refrigerator for a day or two to blend the flavors. When they were reheated, the beans were thick and flavorful.

We didn't spend a lot of additional time or money to add those extra-special touches. However, we got rave reviews from the guests because they're a superior product that was made with care. You know what they said? "*Wow*, these beans are great!" I couldn't have said it better myself.

- Rule #3: Watch the heat!

It's often a great idea to precook your food to save yourself time later. However, there are a couple of things that I want you to take into consideration before you partially cook food ahead of time.

> Slightly *undercook* foods during their precooking stage. Blanching and chilling vegetables, potatoes, pasta, and other foods is okay as long as the cooking process is short. Items should be precooked just until the correct color, or degree of doneness is achieved. The same holds true for items that are grill-marked ahead of time, such as steaks and chops.

> ➤ Reheat precooked items *only* long enough to achieve the proper temperature and desired texture. Food will continue to cook when put into either a warming oven or chafing dish. Overcooking could cause dryness, discoloration, or other quality issues.

- Rule #4: Don't be so tough.

Unless you're talking about jerky, it's no secret that everyone likes beef, pork, lamb, etc. when it's tender. Whether it's a grilled steak or pot roast, the meat *must* be tender in order to satisfy your guests.

Almost anyone can grill a T-bone steak or sauté a veal cutlet and keep it tender (if you can't, you need to practice). The problem arises when you're faced with a braised or simmered meat, such as pot roast, beef stew, or corned beef. Those types of items need long, slow, moist cooking to reach their optimum tenderness.

Sometimes people get impatient and stop cooking braised meats before they're fully tender, which results in a chewy product. Don't do it! Let the meat continue to cook until it's soft and easy to chew. It may take another thirty minutes or two hours, but that extra time makes all the difference between average cooking and really fabulous food.

- Rule #5: Good food needs to *taste* good.

Most caterers offer to serve good food at a fair price—that's no surprise. The truth is, good food at a fair price *just isn't good enough.* You need to serve fantastic food, the kind that gets your customers gushing about your business to their friends. The difference between you and everyone else must be your commitment to proper seasoning.

That's it? Season your food? Yeah, I bet you were expecting some amazing insight from the secret culinary vault. Well, there's no such vault, and it's no secret. Culinarily speaking, proper seasoning is the easiest and most important way to improve your cuisine. What's incredible to me is the fact that not everyone does it. I'm sure you've heard some so-called chef say, "There's salt and pepper on the table if people want to use it." In my opinion, cooks who say that are either making excuses for their laziness or trying to hide their lack of seasoning skills.

Let's face it, if people wanted tasteless, boring food they'd eat at home. Our clients depend on us to serve incredible cuisine; so anything less is a disappointment. To some chefs, seasoning their food is akin to an art form. On the other hand, it doesn't need to be that difficult. In our business, we do it by giving our customers a little something extra—we *exceed their expectations*. The following are some simple examples of how to use additional flavorings to add excitement to your food.

Roasted Meats
Rub with salt, pepper, and minced garlic before roasting.

Sautéed Meats
Sprinkle with salt, pepper, and granulated garlic on *both* sides before sautéing.

Sauces and Gravies
White Sauces: Season with salt and *white* pepper.
> (black pepper has a bug-like appearance that's unappealing to some people)

Brown Sauces: Season with salt, garlic, and black pepper.

Deep-Fried Items
Sprinkle with seasoned salt after frying.

Vegetable Side Dishes
Top with melted butter and slivered red onions; sprinkle with seasoned salt and white pepper.

Mashed Potatoes
Flavor with butter, whole milk, seasoned salt, and white pepper.

Green Salads

Color them up with shredded carrots and red cabbage, diced red peppers, and a touch of thinly sliced red onion.

Macaroni Salad, Coleslaw, Etc.

Season with salt, white pepper, and small amounts of garlic and sugar.

Are you getting the idea? This isn't brain surgery. Season your most basic food items with simple spices and flavorings until you can just barely taste them in the finished product. There are times when you'll want to dazzle your guests with the flavors of one of your specialty dishes, and that's just fine. Yet, you have to remember that most of the time we're flavoring our food for the masses, not your personal taste, so don't overdo it. If you over-season your food, there will be complaints too. Don't risk it.

- Rule #6: Keep the food on the fork!

Maybe you're the kind of person who likes to gnaw on a whole turkey leg, enjoys ten-inch-long noodles in your soup, or cuts a head of lettuce into four wedges before putting the dressing on. That's great for you, but it's unacceptable when preparing food for a catered affair. Remember, we're making food for the masses, and the masses don't like to mess up their clothes or look foolish. Here are a few tips that will save you and your guests some embarrassment.

Watch the finger food: In general, people don't like to touch hot food with their fingers while they're eating. While there are exceptions to this rule, such as chicken pieces, corn on the cob, or pork ribs, for the most part, your guests like to keep their hands clean. Remove the bones or fat from meats and fish that may make them difficult to eat. When making hot sandwiches, don't overfill them to the point where the meat falls into the guests' laps (and they have to put it back on their plate with their fingers, eek!). Think your menu through very carefully and use common sense.

Shorten the spaghetti: It's not only spaghetti; all long pasta should be cut back in length for service. Have you ever tried to twirl a small amount of long spaghetti on your fork and then eat it? If you weren't paying attention, you probably kept twirling until the entire plate began to spin! Then, when you tried to eat it, the spaghetti was so long that you had to slurp it into your mouth. It's fun when you're twelve years old, but not so much when you're an adult wearing formal clothes.

Allowing the pasta to remain long also makes it difficult for the guests to take a smaller portion if necessary, and it could get messy at the buffet table. In addition, when your guests are eating pasta, the fettuccini or linguini *should not* hang down to the bottom of their chin, and drip Alfredo sauce onto their clothes. You're just begging for a complaint.

My solution to this is to break the pasta into manageable lengths before cooking—maybe three to four inches. That will make it easier to serve and eat. Better yet, use shorter pasta to begin with, such as rotini, wagon wheels, or small shells. That way, your Alfredo dish or pasta salad will be safe to eat and interesting, too!

Keep it bite-sized: We've all had the experience of going to the local restaurant and walking up to the salad bar to make a salad. When you arrive, you see a lovely selection of freshly cut produce. Upon closer inspection, you notice that the lettuce was probably chopped using an ax which resulted in three-inch chunks; the cucumber slices are humongous and the tomato wedges are roughly the size of your fist. You'll have to exhaust yourself for twenty minutes trying to cut it all up. Here's another example that you might have experienced. You ordered the French onion soup to go with your meal. It looks and smells great, but once you get past the cheese and crouton, you discover that the chef used the *extra large* onions for this soup and didn't bother to cut them up for you. The long strings of onion cling perilously to the side of the soup spoon, just waiting to drop back into the broth and splash your shirt. By some miracle, you've gotten the spoon up to your mouth and… *oops*, the onion slipped off and is now burning your chin. That isn't too awkward or embarrassing, is it?

So, here's the deal. When serving the public, always cut your vegetables for soups, salads, and side dishes into bite-sized pieces. What it bite-sized? The rule of thumb is don't cut anything larger than will easily fit onto a standard sized fork or soup spoon without falling off. Anything bigger than that is *too big.*

Of course, there are the usual exceptions. Some people like to request whole green beans, asparagus spears, broccoli spears, etc. All you can do is politely explain the negatives and hope for the best.

- Rule #7: Accentuate the positive.

You've finally gotten to this important point. The food is cut, cooked, and seasoned properly, and it really tastes great. Now, it's your job to finish it and make it look even more attractive than it already does. That's where your garnishing skills come into play.

Garnishing makes everything look beautiful and is a fantastic way to exceed expectations. Even though it's an added step, it shouldn't take a lot of extra effort. Oh sure, you may be an excellent vegetable carver who can create the Eiffel Tower out of a carrot. You deserve a pat on the back. However, most of us don't have either the time or the patience for that sort of thing. Plus, it's not really necessary. All you need is a little knowledge and some imagination.

I've had people say to me, "I'd like to do more garnishing, but I'm just not that creative." Who cares? Creativity is really overrated anyway. During the long history of humanity, almost everything you can think of was created by someone else before you. When you do a little research into garnishing techniques, you'll find an enormous amount of information on the subject. Then, you just have to *steal it.* It's completely legal.

Start with catering publications that have great pictures of beautiful buffets. In the photos, pay special attention to the way other caterers use garnishes. Then, simply use those food presentation ideas and techniques to accentuate your own buffets.

Another idea is to get yourself a good garnishing book. There's no need to go overboard with this. Just purchase a book that contains some examples of simple vegetable carvings, including pictures and instructions. You can find a bunch of them online or at the local book store.

Once you have the book, practice a few of the carving techniques in your spare time. You'll be amazed at how easy it is to create beautiful apple birds and tomato roses with a paring knife and a little patience. When you've mastered three or four of them, start to use the garnishes on your upcoming buffets. Put them in the chafing dishes with the food. Arrange them tastefully on the buffet table. Don't be surprised if your decorations receive just as many positive comments as the food. When you're finished with one book, move on to another one. Expand your skills, experiment often, and have fun.

Okay, so you've got severe arthritis, and carving food just isn't your thing. You can still garnish your food beautifully. Many caterers just use fresh flowers to garnish their food. You can do the same thing, though you'll want to avoid the poisonous ones; they tend to put a damper on the party. Florists will provide specific flowers for a price. However, if you want free flowers, there are a couple of options to consider.

If you have a green thumb, you could plant a beautiful flower garden by yourself. That way, you can grow the exact varieties that you like and they'll be ready to harvest continuously throughout the year. The other option is to snip off what you need at the city park. I have done this in an *emergency*, but I'll just let you know that it's frowned upon, so don't get caught!

I hope that the information in this chapter about fabulous food has given you some insight into ways that you can exceed expectations and generate more income through your menu items. I trust that you'll enjoy this aspect of catering as much as I do. I wish you good luck on your culinary journey.

THE BOOK OF MAXIMUM YIELDS

Getting a Bigger Piece of the Pie

The Language of Numbers

In the previous chapter, you learned a little bit about making great food. However, as important as preparing and serving wonderful food is, it won't make one bit of difference if your business can't generate positive income. There's a long line of former caterers who thought they could get by on good food alone, only to have their businesses hit a brick wall when they couldn't turn a profit. Your ability to utilize math skills to positively influence your bottom line will definitely propel you toward catering riches.

Learning math is like learning a second language. Visualize a room full of people at a party. Three individuals are mathematicians, and everyone else has other occupations. The three mathematicians manage to find each other and start a conversation about (what else?) math. At first, the people around them want to be polite and act as if they're interested. One or two brave souls may even try to enter the math conversation. It's all to no avail. Eventually, the three mathematicians have one corner of the room all to themselves. It's not that the other partygoers are being rude; it's just that they don't understand the language. We could use the same example and insert three people who speak French or Russian. The outcome would be the same. So, my question to you is this: "If math is just a language to be learned, then why are so many people afraid of it?" You don't hear of anyone being petrified of learning Spanish or German (at least I haven't). It's natural to be a little nervous when learning a new language, but *petrified*? I doubt it.

Math anxiety or fear of math is actually quite common. It's very similar to stage fright. Why does someone suffer stage fright? Is it the fear of being embarrassed in front of a crowd? Fear of not remembering some lines of dialogue? Fear of being judged as stupid? Math anxiety conjures up that same type of fear. For the most part, math anxiety is the fear of doing the math *incorrectly*—our minds draw a blank, and we think we'll fail. Of course, the more frustrated and anxious our minds become, the greater the chance we'll draw blanks. It's an endless cycle of frustration. I have two words for everyone out there who absolutely *hates* math—*chill out!* Take some deep breaths. Switch to decaf coffee if necessary. From this moment on, basic math skills are going to be your best friend, because of their ability to open your eyes to hidden riches.

The language of numbers has so many significant things to tell us. It tells us how much we'll get from our paychecks after taxes and what our income tax refund will be. It helps us to understand when our final mortgage payment will be due and how much we'll pay for new shoes that are 30 percent off.

For us in the catering business, math tells us how much food to prepare and what our weekly labor cost percentage is. But, the most important reason for learning basic math skills is:

Knowing and understanding basic food service math is the third *nonnegotiable, absolutely essential* part of running a catering business that attracts big money.

How do I know this? Because when you examine any of the oodles of books dealing with how to run a successful catering business, virtually all of them mention it. Some books will tell you to *pay attention* to food cost, while others point out the importance of *knowing* your food cost. The problem is, nearly all of these books will allow you to figure out the rest all by yourself. They won't actually tell you how to *calculate* your food cost.

One reason for this is that calculating food costs is a pretty involved process that's sometimes difficult to explain. Food service math is a completely different animal, but it doesn't have to be ferocious. As your personal tutor in the principles of profitable catering, difficult concepts don't scare me. What does frighten me is allowing potential rich caterers, such as yourself, to go out into the catering world and operate their businesses without the tools necessary for ultimate success. For that reason, I'm going to help you to understand how to make money at the most basic level of the business. Once you can do that, the rest will be a piece of cake.

So, you and I are going to slog through the dark jungle of food service mathematics. With machetes in hand, we're going to slice away all of the doubt and confusion about food costing. In this particular book, we'll study measurements, recipe conversions, and yield testing. In "The Book of Calculated Riches," we'll study ingredient costing, recipe costing, and menu pricing. "The Book of Profitable Portions" includes sections on portion sizes, accurate counting, and kitchen waste. The final math-related chapter, "The

Book of Savvy Purchasing," covers food ordering, buying in bulk, and menu flexibility. Each book is filled with detailed explanations and simple formulas to help make learning these concepts much easier—I guarantee it.

When reading the books I mention above, I encourage you take as much time as you need and digest everything very slowly. There's no reason to hurry through it. Review each section as many times as it takes to comprehend it fully and then move on. When you've finished, you should have a complete understanding of the concepts necessary to create a booming business.

A Measured Way to Riches

A very good indicator of your success as a caterer is your ability to measure. You can't become a rich caterer without knowing pounds, ounces, cups, teaspoons, gallons, and so on. How well do you know your measurements? Let's take a little test to find out. Fill in the blanks below to see if you know the correct answers. Don't cheat!

- There are _____ teaspoons in a tablespoon.
- There are _____ cups in a quart.
- There are _____ volume ounces in a cup.
- There are _____ quarts in a gallon.
- There are _____ weight ounces in a pound.

Those were pretty easy, weren't they? Or were they? We'll look up the answers in a second. Now fill in the blanks for this next set of statements using your answers from above.

- 24 teaspoons equals _____ tablespoons.
- 14 cups equals _____ quarts.
- 72 volume ounces equal _____ cups.
- 26 quarts equals _____ gallons.
- 240 weight ounces equals _____ pounds.

How many of those conversions were you able to correctly calculate by using the first set of numbers? I'm guessing that they gave you a little trouble. Many people, even if they know the smaller answers in the first set of statements, have trouble with the second set. How come? Because the smaller numbers are often memorized, so you don't have to think too much. The larger numbers require some higher level thinking and basic math skills. Okay, go ahead and look at the answers in figure 4.1 and see how many you actually got correct.

Figure 4.1

There are three teaspoons in a tablespoon.

There are four cups in a quart.

There are eight volume ounces in a cup.

There are four quarts in a gallon.

There are sixteen weight ounces in a pound.

Twenty-four teaspoons are equal to eight tablespoons.

Fourteen cups are equal to three and a half quarts.

Seventy-two volume ounces are equal to nine cups.

26 quarts equals 6 ½ gallons.

240 weight ounces equals 15 pounds

Now, I know what you folks with math phobia might be thinking. "Do we really need to know this to be successful? How often are we going to use these skills, anyway?" Let me give you an example that answers those questions.

Imagine that you have a catered event this weekend for six hundred people. You'll be preparing a soup recipe that makes ten portions and calls for one teaspoon of hot pepper sauce as an ingredient. Obviously you'll need to increase the recipe. To convert it, you take six hundred people and divide that number by ten portions per recipe, which equals sixty (I'll explain this in detail shortly). That means you must increase the recipe sixty times for this event. The initial one teaspoon of hot pepper sauce has now become sixty teaspoons for the larger recipe. Your cook is positive that there are two teaspoons in every tablespoon (a common mistake), and makes the calculation. It looks like this:

Sixty teaspoons divided by two (number of teaspoons *believed* to be in a tablespoon) = thirty tablespoons of hot pepper sauce.

In reality, there are three teaspoons per tablespoon, and the calculation should look like this:

Sixty teaspoons divided by three (number of *actual* teaspoons in a tablespoon) = twenty tablespoons of hot pepper sauce.

Oops! You've just put an extra ten tablespoons of atomic heat into your soup. What are you going to do *now?* If you caught the mistake in time, you could make another batch of soup. However, I'm guessing that you really don't want to make a second batch of soup for six hundred people. Think of all the extra time and money you'd be wasting to cover that error.

Even worse, you might not catch the mistake and serve the soup to your guests. I understand that *some* people may enjoy spicy soup, but I can assure you that others would complain about it. It might even be the client who's paying the bill for the event. What kind of word-of-mouth advertising will you be getting from this dilemma? Not good, I promise you.

A caterer performs hundreds of minor math calculations for each large event. As you can see, a small mistake in the beginning of the process could turn into a big problem later. The previous example was for *one* ingredient in *one* recipe. A single catered event may require *dozens* of different recipes. These recipes contain *hundreds* of ingredients, and everything needs to be converted properly for it all to work. Do you see what I mean? One or two blunders like this could spell disaster for your business. Rich caterers don't take that chance.

In order to avoid costly errors, you'll need to know basic weight and volume measurements inside and out. Memorize the measurements chart below (figure 4.2) and practice those calculations until they're perfect. Give the measurements chart to your staff as well, so that everyone can be on the same page. Your effort to understand and use correct measurements *now* will pay extensive dividends down the road.

Figure 4.2

Volume Measures							
3 teaspoons	=	1 tablespoon					
2 tablespoons	=	1 ounce					
4 tablespoons	=	1/4 cup					
8 tablespoons	=	1/2 cup					
12 tablespoons	=	3/4 cup					
1 cup	=	8 ounces	=	16 tablespoons			
1 pint	=	2 cups	=	16 ounces			
1 quart	=	4 cups	=	2 pints	=	32 ounces	
1 gallon	=	4 quarts	=	16 cups	=	128 ounces	

Weight Measures

1 pound = 16 ounces

Conversions Are Crucial

Correct recipe conversions are an essential part of your basic math skills. If you can't increase or decrease ingredient amounts properly, you'll be doomed to having either too many leftovers or not enough food to satisfy your clients. Both of those situations are unacceptable. In order to convert recipes properly, you need to understand one simple formula:

New yield divided by old yield = conversion factor

The old yield is the number of portions that a recipe currently makes. The new yield is the number of portions that you want to convert it to. The conversion factor is the *number of times larger or smaller* the new yield is. How does this all work? We'll start with something simple. Take a look at the recipe listed below:

Perfect Lemonade Recipe

Ingredients:
1 cup sugar
1 cup lemon juice (5 lemons)
6 cups cold water

By adding up the ingredients in the recipe, you can see that it makes eight cups (1 cup + 1 cup + 6 cups). If your portion size is 8 ounces (1 cup), then the recipe yields eight portions.

Imagine that you have an event booked for tomorrow night and need enough lemonade for 240 portions. The formula works like this:

New yield divided by old yield = conversion factor
240 portions ÷ 8 portions = 30

Now that you have the conversion factor, all you do is multiply each ingredient by thirty to come up with the right amount. Let's do it:

Perfect Lemonade Recipe

Old Amounts	Converted Amounts
1 cup sugar	x 30 = 30 cups sugar
1 cup lemon juice (5 lemons)	x 30 = 30 cups lemon juice (150 lemons)
6 cups cold water	x 30 = 180 cups cold water
Total yield: 2 quarts/8 portions	Total yield: 15 gallons/240 portions

That's all there is to it. Pretty simple, isn't it? Notice that I also converted the total yields to quarts and gallons using the previous measurements chart. The recipe conversion formula also works the same way if the recipe needs to be converted to a smaller number of portions. Using the same recipe, let's convert it down to four portions.

New yield divided by old yield = conversion factor
4 portions ÷ 8 portions = .50

Again, simply multiply each ingredient by .50 to come up with the amount of each ingredient necessary to make lemonade for four people.

Perfect Lemonade Recipe

Old Amounts		Converted Amounts
1 cup sugar	x .50 =	.50 (1/2) cup sugar
1 cup lemon juice	x .50 =	.50 (1/2) cup lemon juice
6 cups cold water	x .50 =	3 cups cold water
Total yield: 2 quarts/8 portions		Total yield: 1 quart/4 portions

To tell you the truth, I don't know if this lemonade recipe is good or not, but it doesn't matter. What's important is that you understand the formula for recipe conversion and can use it like a pro. Once you've mastered it, you can put one more tool in your rich caterer toolbox.

Mind your APs and EPs

Knowing about APs and EPs is not only important to your bottom line; it also makes food ordering easier and less stressful. You're probably wondering exactly what APs and EPs are.

AP and EP weights are used to designate the stage of preparation for a particular food item. Although these weights can refer to many food products, they're most often used for fruits and vegetables. AP stands for "as purchased," and it means the weight of a food product as it's delivered by the supplier. For example, I'm making a large amount of creamy coleslaw for an event next week and have ordered a fifty-pound case of cabbage from my vegetable supplier. When the cabbage arrives, I weigh it and see that it weighs exactly fifty pounds. It is then stored in my walk-in cooler until preparation time. The cabbage I've just received weighs fifty pounds *AP (as purchased)*.

A few days later, I'm going to get the cabbage ready for the coleslaw by performing a few simple pre-preparation techniques. First, I'll remove the tough outer leaves until I get to the useable cabbage. Next, I'll cut out the core and trim any blemishes that I find on the surface. The remaining cabbage is now said to be *EP (edible portion)*, because all of it can be eaten. I now put my trimmed cabbage on the scale, and it weighs forty pounds. You can see that its weight is significantly different from when it arrived. Almost every fruit or vegetable has both an AP weight and an EP weight, because they need to be trimmed, peeled, or further processed before being eaten.

Why is this important to you? Because if a recipe calls for twenty pounds of chopped onions EP, and you purchase twenty pounds of onions AP, you'll end up with fewer onions than you need, because of trimming loss. On the other hand, if your recipe calls for an AP amount and you mistake it for an EP amount, you'll be buying *more* onions than you need. By making this boo-boo, you could end up with a large amount of extra product. It's a simple waste of money. Rich caterers just don't make this mistake. You must know and use the *yield percentage* for every fruit and vegetable when you do your produce ordering.

What, you may ask, is a *yield percentage*? Each fruit and vegetable has its own specific trimming loss, which leaves a certain amount of the item left to be eaten. Again, let's use onions as an example, since they're used so often in recipes. Our onion is large, and it weighs twelve ounces. To find the yield percentage of this onion, trim off the excess skin and any unusable parts. When we put the remaining edible portion on the scale, the EP weight is 10.8 ounces. Now we need to find out what percentage of the onion is left over after trimming. This is called the yield percentage. Here's the formula to correctly calculate the yield percentage:

EP weight divided by AP weight = yield percentage

In our case, the calculation would look like this:

10.8 ounces ÷ 12 ounces = .90 or 90%

The onion that we've just tested has a *yield percentage* of 90 percent.

You may be wondering if you have to do these calculations for *every* single onion that you use. Before you start making plans to burn this book, let me assure you that you *do not*. Each onion has about the same percentage of trimming waste, so, logically it would have nearly the same yield percentage as well (around 90 percent).

Another similar question may come out of your mouth: "Do I have to make these calculations for *every* fruit and vegetable that I use?" Once again, the answer is no. The yield percentages for the most common fruits and vegetables are available in the appendix of this volume (you're welcome). If you come across one that isn't listed, figure it out yourself, and add it to the list. The extra time you spend will be worth it, and you only have to do it once. Now that you understand what yield percentages are, I'm going to show you how to use them.

First, when you look at your recipes, decide if the amounts are listed as AP or EP measurements. If they're AP, that's fine, no other calculations are needed. If the amounts are EP, you'll need to convert them before you order the food. The following is an example of how to convert EP amounts into AP amounts for purchasing. My recipe for carrot salad calls for these ingredient amounts:

Carrot Salad Recipe

10 pounds shredded carrots
2 pounds raisins
3 pounds chopped apples
5 cups mayonnaise
1 tablespoon salt
½ teaspoon white pepper

For this recipe, all of the fresh fruits and vegetables have been trimmed, and the listed amounts are regarded as EP weights. Raisins, mayonnaise, salt, and white pepper don't require any trimming and need no further calculations. Mark the ingredient amounts as EP where necessary.

Carrot Salad Recipe

10 pounds shredded carrots EP
2 pounds raisins
3 pounds chopped apples EP
5 cups mayonnaise
1 tablespoon salt
½ teaspoon white pepper

Now comes the important part: changing the recipe amounts to AP weights for accurate ordering. Use the following formula to change EPs into APs:

EP weight divided by yield percentage = AP weight

The yield percentage for carrots is about 80 percent so let's plug the numbers into the formula:

EP weight divided by yield percentage = AP weight

10 pounds ÷ 80% or .80 = 12.50 pounds

The formula is telling you that you must order 12.50 or 12 ½ pounds of carrots in order to arrive at 10 pounds EP. The same calculation must be done for the apples. The yield percentage for apples is about 75 percent:

EP weight divided by yield percentage = AP weight

3 pounds ÷ 75% or .75 = 4 pounds

In order to end up with three pounds of diced apples EP, you should obtain four pounds from your supplier.

At this point, you would write down the amount of carrots and apples you need to order on your shopping list. Once you have done this for all your recipes, you're ready to submit your master order list to the supplier.

I hope you can see how important it is to mind your APs and EPs. Rich caterers find that it's indispensable information for accurate supply ordering.

"Watch the Pennies and the Dollars Take Care of Themselves."

That's what one of my culinary school instructors repeatedly said to us. I listened to him, too, because he was teaching us about meat—one of the most expensive ingredients that we'll use as caterers.

The math that's used to calculate accurate meat amounts and costs is very similar to that of fruits and vegetables. There is trimming loss involved for all three of those categories of ingredients. The big difference is, if you make a mistake with fruits and vegetables, the money lost probably won't take all of your profits.

However, if you make a math mistake with the meat entrees, you might lose money on the event, and that's unacceptable.

As with fruits and vegetables, if you don't know what the EP weights for your meat items are, there might not be enough food to serve your guests. Have you ever been one of the last people to walk up to a buffet table, only to find that one of the menu items has run out? How did you feel? If it's a salad, potato, or vegetable, you might have felt a bit slighted. On the other hand, if it was one of the meat entrees, you probably felt the urge to give the caterer a piece of your mind. That's exactly how your clients are going to feel, and they'll come straight to *you* for an explanation.

Running short of meat on a buffet that's designed to show off your business is inexcusable. Keeping your clients happy and making a good profit on the meat items you serve begins with proper ordering. A raw meat yield test is a great way to insure this. Initially, a raw meat yield test requires three things: the name of the meat item, the AP weight, and the cost per pound.

As a simple example, let's buy a whole Beef Eye Round and trim it. Most meat items that you order these days are put in clear plastic packaging and vacuum packed to retain freshness. So, the most logical thing to do is weigh the meat item *in the packaging* first, to get an accurate AP weight. When we put the packaged eye round on the scale, we see that it weighs 6.50 pounds. Next, on a three-by-five index card, write the item name, AP weight, and AP cost per pound (from the supplier's invoice) just like this:

Meat item:	Beef Eye Round
AP weight:	6.50 pounds
AP cost per pound:	$2.60

Depending on the cut of meat, you may have to trim off fat, bones, connective tissue, cartilage, and more before getting to the edible portion. Some cuts of meat need more trimming than others. The eye round that we've chosen for this yield test will require minimal trimming. Let's cut open the packaging and carefully trim the fat and connective tissue from the eye round until it meets our specifications. The cooking method (roasting, braising, broiling, etc.) will determine the amount of trimming that we'll do. Once the trimming is finished, we weigh the eye round again. This time, the eye round has an EP weight of 5.50 pounds. Write that on the card:

Meat item:	**Beef Eye Round**
AP weight:	6.50 pounds
AP cost per pound:	$2.60
EP weight:	5.50 pounds

Now it's time to find out the cost per pound of the trimmed eye round. You may think that the cost per pound is still $2.60. Many *ex*-caterers have made that same mistake (at their peril). Rich caterers know that there's a difference. Follow along carefully as I explain this to you.

The first step is to calculate the total cost of the entire piece of meat. Supermarkets do this with their individual packages of meat. To do it, you need to simply multiply the AP weight times the AP cost per pound. It looks like this:

AP weight multiplied by
AP cost per pound = total cost of the meat

6.50 pounds (6 ½) x $2.60 = $16.90

Great! You've now calculated the total cost for 6.50 pounds of eye round. Write it down on your card so that we can use it later:

Meat item:	**Beef Eye Round**
AP weight:	6.50 pounds
AP cost per pound:	$2.60
EP weight:	5.50 pounds
Total cost:	$16.90

But wait, we threw away the worthless trimmings and only have 5.50 pounds of meat left. Unfortunately, suppliers don't give you a rebate on the scraps that you don't use. So, actually, the cost is $16.90 for only 5.50 pounds of edible meat. That means the cost per pound has just gone up. In order to calculate the *new* cost per pound, you must take the total cost of the meat and divide it by the EP weight.

Total cost of meat divided by EP weight = EP cost per pound

$$\$16.90 \div 5.50 \text{ pounds } (5 \tfrac{1}{2}) = \$3.08 \ (3.072)$$

Congratulations! You now know one of the most important math calculations in this book. I hope that you were able to follow along. If not, keep trying until you do. Comparing the old and new costs per pound, can you see what a big difference it makes to use the correct cost when pricing your menu? Use the new cost, and you're on your way to becoming a rich caterer; use the old one, and your business goes spiraling downward. Write the new cost per pound on the three-by-five card:

Meat item:	**Beef Eye Round**
AP weight:	6.50 pounds
AP cost per pound:	$2.60
EP weight:	5.50 pounds
Total cost:	$16.90
EP cost per pound:	$3.08

As you inch this book closer to the shredder, you're probably asking, "Do I have to do this trimming test for every single eye round that I use?" The answer is *absolutely not*. As long as the same cut of meat is trimmed in basically the same way every time, you don't need to perform another trimming test. The percentage of unusable trim will stay about the same for each specific cut of meat. In other words, the yield percentage for Beef Eye Round will remain relatively constant from eye round, to eye round, to eye round.

However, we both know that the price of meat fluctuates over time. In order to compensate for that, you need to perform one more calculation to arrive at a *conversion factor*.

Conversion factor? Didn't we use that when we converted recipes? Yes, as a matter of fact, we did, and it works in the same way. All you have to do is divide the EP cost per pound by the AP cost per pound like this:

EP cost per pound divided by
AP cost per pound = EP conversion factor

$3.08 ÷ $2.60 = 1.19 (1.184)

Now write the conversion factor on your three-by-five card:

Meat item:	Beef Eye Round
AP weight:	6.50 pounds
AP cost per pound:	$2.60
EP weight:	5.50 pounds
Total cost:	$16.90
EP cost per pound:	$3.08
EP conversion factor:	1.19

Okay, here's the magical part. Whenever you order more eye rounds, check the price and multiply it by the conversion factor to get the new, edible portion, cost per pound. For example, today I need to buy more eye rounds for roast beef. The price quoted for eye rounds by my supplier is $2.79 per pound. Here's the calculation:

Quoted price per pound multiplied by
EP conversion factor = EP cost per pound

$2.79 x 1.19 = $3.32

Now, let's say that the price of eye rounds has gone *down* this week. Does the formula work the same way? It sure does. Try it again using $2.29 per pound as your quoted price.

Quoted price per pound multiplied by
EP conversion factor = EP cost per pound

$2.29 x 1.19 = $2.73

It works like a charm. The beauty is, you can use this same conversion factor for Beef Eye Round next week or five years from now. It will never change.

Remember, the raw meat yield test is only for items that have AP and EP weights. You can rule out meats that are already portion cut or don't require trimming before preparation. The idea is to perform a raw yield test on every trimmed meat item that you have on your menu. This would probably amount to only about a dozen items. If it's more than that, so what? Isn't it valuable to know that you're making all of the money possible from the meat items on your menu?

Now that you've done some great work and completed the raw meat yield test, I think it's time for a mental break. Take a few deep breaths, put the book down, and relax your brain. A pause here for a drink and snack might be a good idea. I'll get back with you in about twenty minutes.

(Pause for well-deserved math-less intermission.)

Okay, welcome back! Once again, I'm going to show you some vital information that will help you improve the accuracy of your food ordering and menu pricing. This tool is the rich caterer's pal, and it's called the *cooked* meat yield test.

Think about the eye round that we performed the raw meat yield test on. If you remember correctly, the EP weight of the trimmed roast was 5.50 pounds. We're now going to make this item into pot roast and complete a cooked meat yield test to see how much the meat shrinks during cooking.

As we all know (or maybe not), a pot roast is seared on all sides and cooked with liquid until it's tender. During the time that the roast is in the pot, it loses a considerable amount of weight because of moisture loss. This cooking loss is called *shrinkage*. The purpose of the cooked meat yield test is to tell us what amount of shrinkage occurs during cooking so that we can calculate the increased cost per pound of the finished product.

As with the raw meat yield test, you'll need to write the information you find on a three-by-five card. I'm going to use the same one as before, that way I have all of my important information for this menu item in one place.

Let's begin by cooking the eye round as a pot roast until it's tender. Remove the pot roast from the pot and let it drain for a few minutes. When it has cooled slightly, put the roast on the scale to measure the cooked weight. Our roast weighs 3.70 pounds after cooking. I'll write that down on the previous three-by-five card and add "pot roast" to the top. It looks like this:

Meat item:	Beef Eye Round/Pot Roast	
AP weight:	6.50 pounds	Cooked weight: 3.70 pounds
AP cost per pound:	$2.60	
EP weight:	5.50 pounds	
Total cost:	$16.90	
EP cost per pound:	$3.08	
EP conversion factor:	1.19	

Believe it or not, we're now paying $16.90 for only 3.70 pounds of cooked meat. The next step is to find out the cost per pound of the cooked pot roast. To do this, take the total cost and divide it by the cooked weight. Here's the formula:

Total cost of meat divided by
cooked weight = cooked cost per pound

$16.90 ÷ 3.70 pounds = $4.57 (4.567)

Wow, no wonder cooked sandwich meats are so expensive in supermarket delis! Once again, can you see what a big difference it makes to use the correct cost per pound when pricing your menu? Rich caterers can. Write the cooked cost per pound on your card.

Meat item:	Beef Eye Round/Pot Roast	
AP weight:	6.50 pounds	Cooked weight: 3.70 pounds
AP cost per pound:	$2.60	Cooked cost per pound: $4.57
EP weight:	5.50 pounds	
Total cost:	$16.90	
EP cost per pound:	$3.08	
EP conversion factor: 1.19		

Now let's calculate the final conversion factor for cooked meat. It's done the same way as the previous EP conversion factor, replacing the EP cost per pound with the cooked cost per pound. Take a look at the formula:

Cooked cost per pound divided by
AP cost per pound = cooked conversion factor

$4.57 ÷ $2.60 per pound = 1.76 (1.757)

Finally, add the cooked conversion factor to your card:

Meat item:	Beef Eye Round/Pot Roast	
AP weight:	6.50 pound	Cooked weight: 3.70 pounds
AP cost per pound:	$2.59	Cooked cost per pound: $4.57
EP weight:	5.50 pounds	Cooked conversion factor: 1.76
Total cost:	$16.90	
EP cost per pound:	$3.08	
EP conversion factor:	1.19	

You can use this cooked conversion factor the same way that you used the EP conversion factor. That same formula will show you what the cost per pound of your cooked pot roast is whenever the price of eye round goes up or down.

This cooked yield test is used mostly with roasted and braised meat items. You'll need to identify the specific menu items that need to be tested. Fortunately, as with the raw meat yield test, you only need to test each menu item once, and you can use the information over a lifetime of catering. I suggest that you make a three-by-five card like this for every meat item on your menu and keep them in a file box in the office. Then they'll always be at your fingertips for easy reference. In addition, document this data on your computer as a back-up. That way you can retrieve it easily when someone (perhaps you) accidentally knocks your file box into the trash and it's never seen again.

One last thing about cooking loss: the amount of shrinkage will vary depending on the cut of meat used and the amount of cooking done to it. A cut of meat cooked rare will have very little cooking loss, while meats cooked well-done, or soft, will lose quite a bit. Because of this, you'll need to be smart about using precise cooking loss percentages whenever you order meat for any event.

Un-Shrinking the Shrinkage

Let me give you an example of how shrinkage affects your ordering. Let's say that you're going to serve that eye round pot roast to one hundred people. When it comes time to order, you'll need to figure out how much total meat you'll need to prepare to serve a group that size. You figure that each person will eat about six ounces (cooked weight) of pot roast. So, you make the calculation as follows:

Number of ounces per person multiplied by
number of people = total ounces needed

6 ounces pot roast x 100 people = 600 ounces

Now you divide the total ounces by sixteen (ounces in one pound) in order to calculate the number of pounds of cooked meat needed for one hundred people:

Total ounces divided by number of
ounces per pound = number of pounds needed

600 ounces ÷ 16 = 37.5 pounds

There you go. Just order 37.5 pounds of meat and it's all good, right? *Wrong*. You forgot to compensate for the moisture loss during cooking—the *shrinkage*. Next, you must calculate the number of pounds of raw meat that you'll need to buy in order arrive at the final *cooked* weight of 37.5 pounds.

To put it simply (I think): You already know the shrunk weight—now un-shrink it!

In order to do that, you must take the final cooked weight and divide it by the original raw AP weight on your index card. This will show you the yield percentage for the pot roast. Let's use our previous index card weights to illustrate this:

Meat item: Beef Eye Round/Pot Roast

AP weight:	6.50 pounds	Cooked weight:	3.70 pounds
AP cost per pound:	$2.59	Cooked cost per pound:	$4.57
EP weight:	5.50 pounds	Cooked conversion factor:	1.76
Total cost:	$16.90		
EP cost per pound:	$3.08		
EP conversion factor:	1.19		

For one piece of eye round pot roast, the raw, AP weight was 6.50 pounds, and the final cooked weight was 3.70 pounds. Take the amounts for that one piece and figure out the yield percentage by using the previously mentioned formula:

Final cooked weight divided by AP weight = yield percentage

3.70 pounds ÷ 6.50 pounds = 56.9% (.5692)

That means, of the original 6.50 pounds of eye round that you started with, only 56.9 percent will be served to guests. That's quite a loss, but not unusual for fully cooked meats that have been trimmed. Just so we don't forget it, let's write that percentage on our index card.

Meat item:	**Beef Eye Round/Pot Roast**	
AP weight:	6.50 pounds	Cooked weight: 3.70 pound
AP cost per pound:	$2.59	Cooked cost per pound: $4.57
EP weight:	5.50 pounds	Cooked conversion factor: 1.76
Total cost:	$16.90	Cooked yield percentage: 56.9%
EP cost per pound:	$3.08	
EP conversion factor:	1.19	

You'll need one more formula before you can calculate the amount of meat to order for those one hundred people. Take the final cooked weight and divide it by the yield percentage to arrive at the amount of raw meat that must be ordered. Why don't we try it with the original numbers to see if it works?

Final cooked weight divided by yield percentage = AP weight

3.70 pounds ÷ 56.9% (.569) = 6.50 pounds (6.502)

Yep, that worked just fine, so let's get back to that meal for one hundred people. Since you need 37.5 pounds of cooked pot roast for the event, plug that number in for the final cooked weight, and use the same yield percentage. The answer you get will be the number of pounds of raw meat that you should order for the event. Here we go:

Final cooked weight divided by yield percentage = AP weight

37.50 pounds ÷ 56.9% (.569) = 66.25 pounds (66.254)

With the final calculation completed, it is now clear that you'll need to order at least 66.25 pounds of raw eye round for the event. I always order five to ten extra pounds to compensate for losses from slicing. It also covers me just in case Bert, my butterfingered staff member, drops a serving or two on the floor.

When I'm using meat that doesn't require trimming and is cooked well-done, I use a standard yield percentage of 66 percent. That means that for every ten pounds of raw meat, such as ground beef or stew meat, there is a cooked yield of approximately 6.60 pounds.

Keep track of your yield percentages for every meat item that you serve. Write them on your index cards, and refer to them often when ordering. This hard work of calculating yield percentages will pay off in cash when you put it into practice.

THE BOOK OF CALCULATED RICHES
The Basics of Costing and Pricing

Food Costing 101: Ingredient Costing for Rich Caterers

Costing out recipe ingredients is a fundamental part of catering success. When you're unaware of what menu items cost, you can't really be sure if you're making a profit. Beyond that, keeping an eye on your ingredient costs on a regular basis will enable you to spot large increases or decreases in price. When prices increase, you can find another supplier or substitute a lower-priced ingredient. When prices decrease, you may consider stocking up on sale items for later use. Either way, you help your business.

Creating a recipe book of your menu items is also a great idea. You can keep one copy for kitchen use and another to help with food costing. Your best bet is to have the recipes entered on a computer and then backed-up for safe keeping. If you're not good at typing or just don't have the time, pay someone else to enter them for you and double-check the documents when they're completed. Print the recipes and either laminate them or cover them with plastic sheet protectors. When finished, organize the recipes in a sturdy binder according to categories, such as soups, appetizers, main courses, etc. If possible, insert a photo of the finished item with each recipe for ease of identification. All of these little steps take time initially but will save time and training later on. Once you've completed the recipe book, you're ready to move on to costing.

To start with, I'll let you know that there are various software programs that will help you with ingredient costing. If you purchase one and figure out how to use it, you might be able to do the calculations faster. You'll have to decide if the time saved is worth the price. In the mean time, let's begin by describing the tried and true method.

The first thing you'll need to do is to create a list of the ingredients from your new recipe book. Proceed in order, from recipe to recipe, until you've listed all of the ingredients. There's no need to be too fussy at this stage, because you're going to organize everything again later. When you're finished, create a set of pages or charts that look similar to figure 5.1.

Figure 5.1

CATEGORY	AP COST $	AP UNIT	UNIT 1	COST PER UNIT 1	UNIT 2	COST PER UNIT 2	UNIT 3	COST PER UNIT 3
DRY INGREDIENTS								
CANNED GOODS								
DAIRY PRODUCTS								
FROZEN FOOD								

CATEGORY	AP COST $	AP UNIT	UNIT 1	COST PER UNIT 1	UNIT 2	COST PER UNIT 2	UNIT 3	COST PER UNIT 3
MEAT								
POULTRY								
SEAFOOD								
FRESH PRODUCE								
DISPOSABLE ITEMS								

When you've completed the rows, fill in the columns with the items from your ingredient list, as shown in figure 5.2. Make sure that you organize them into the correct categories.

Figure 5.2

CATEGORY	AP COST $	AP UNIT	UNIT 1	COST PER UNIT 1	UNIT 2	COST PER UNIT 2	UNIT 3	COST PER UNIT 3
DRY INGREDIENTS								
Salt								
White pepper								
Sugar								
All-purpose flour								
Bread crumbs								
Raisins								
CANNED GOODS								
Peaches, 35–40 count								
White vinegar								
Vegetable oil								
Honey								
Artichoke hearts								
Mayonnaise								
DAIRY PRODUCTS								
Whole milk								
Chocolate milk								
Heavy cream								
Shredded cheddar								
Large eggs								
FROZEN FOOD								
Vanilla ice cream								
Peas								
French fries								
Pie shells								

CATEGORY	AP COST $	AP UNIT	UNIT 1	COST PER UNIT 1	UNIT 2	COST PER UNIT 2	UNIT 3	COST PER UNIT 3
MEATS								
Ground beef								
Eye rounds								
Lamb rack								
Pork chops, bone-in								
Bacon, 14–18 count								
POULTRY								
Chicken breasts, 6 ounce								
Turkey cutlets								
Cornish hens								
Diced chicken								
SEAFOOD								
Cod fillets, 8 ounce								
Shrimp, 16–20 count								
Salmon sides								
Imitation crab								
FRESH PRODUCE								
Yellow onions								
Green onions								
Celery								
Carrots								
Apples								
DISPOSABLES								
Soufflé cups, 4 ounce								
Souffle cup lid								
Plastic wrap, 18-inch								
Foil, 18-inch								
Punch cups								

Some items will fit into multiple categories, such as cod fillets, which are both seafood *and* frozen food. Put these items where it makes the most sense *for you* and where you'll find them the easiest. You may realize at some point that you'll need to add extra lines in some categories. That's fine; add as many lines as necessary to accommodate your many ingredients. Sometimes, you may even require additional categories to reflect the items on your menu. Do whatever it takes. This is *your* ingredient costing chart, so make it easy for *you* to understand.

Next, either check your current invoices or your supplier's pricing sheets to obtain an up-to-date price for the ingredients you've listed. Many vendors have websites available as well. Using a vendor's website allows you to research prices in the vendor's entire catalog. As you find the information, enter the AP costs and AP units in the appropriate columns. Refer to figure 5.3 for an illustration.

You'll notice that there are disposable items included on the charts. The reason for this is simple. You'll be paying for these items too and must consider that expense when costing out your recipes. Will you be putting salad dressings or mayonnaise in portion cups for some of your caterings? Will you be wrapping sandwiches or vegetable pizzas individually with plastic wrap for service during outdoor buffets? Will your wedding punch be served in disposable plastic cups? If so, then those expenses must be accounted for.

Take-out catering uses an enormous amount of disposables and is especially vulnerable to hidden costs. Consider adding the expense of plastic wrap and disposable trays to the cost of party platters. Include the expense of disposable aluminum pans and foil when calculating the cost of hot appetizers or entrees for take-out. Even adhesive labels for identification or heating instructions will cost you a considerable amount of money. If you're able to add those expenses in at the recipe costing stage, you don't have to account for them later. This will save you both time and money.

Some people may think that I'm nit-picking here, but I certainly don't. The most successful caterers consider all costs when running their business and compensate for them whenever possible. If you want to become a rich caterer, then you should do the same.

Figure 5.3

CATEGORY	AP COST $	AP UNIT	UNIT 1	COST PER UNIT 1	UNIT 2	COST PER UNIT 2	UNIT 3	COST PER UNIT 3
DRY INGREDIENTS								
Salt	$15.20	24–26 ounce						
White pepper	$20.12	18 ounce						
Sugar	$29.20	50 pound bag						
All-purpose flour	$10.89	50 pound bag						
Bread crumbs	$22.10	20 pound case						
Raisins	$52.25	12/2 pound box						
CANNED GOODS								
Peaches, 35–40 count	$37.61	6/#10 can						
White vinegar	$16.65	4/1 gallon						
Vegetable oil	$8.74	1 gallon						
Honey	$16.85	5 pound jug						
Artichoke hearts	$28.45	12/14 ounce						
Mayonnaise	$26.80	4/1 gallon						
DAIRY PRODUCTS								
Whole milk	$14.15	4/1 gallon						
Chocolate milk	$13.40	4/1 gallon						
Heavy cream	$3.00	1 quart						
Shredded cheddar	$11.55	5 pound bag						
Large eggs	$16.50	Case/15 dozen						
FROZEN FOOD								
Vanilla ice cream	$17.35	3 gallon						
Peas	$32.40	30 pound case						
French fries	$30.30	6/5 pound bag						
Pie shells	$31.65	case of 24						

CATEGORY	AP COST $	AP UNIT	UNIT 1	COST PER UNIT 1	UNIT 2	COST PER UNIT 2	UNIT 3	COST PER UNIT 3
MEATS								
Ground beef	$41.85	20 pound case						
Eye rounds	—	12/6 pounds each	pound	2.54				
Lamb rack	—	8/2 pounds each	pound	9.445				
Pork chops, bone-in	$33.95	27/6 ounces each						
Bacon, 14–18 count	$35.40	15 pound case						
POULTRY								
Chicken breasts, 6 ounce	$23.70	10 pound case						
Turkey cutlets	$60.70	40/4 ounces each						
Cornish hens	$86.94	case of 24						
Diced chicken	$37.60	10 pound case						
SEAFOOD								
Cod fillets, 8 ounce	$53.20	10 pound case						
Shrimp, 16–20 count	$136.90	20 pound case						
Salmon sides	—	3/2–3 pounds each	pound	11.28				
Imitation crab	$98.99	24 pound case						

CATEGORY	AP COST $	AP UNIT	UNIT 1	COST PER UNIT 1	UNIT 2	COST PER UNIT 2	UNIT 3	COST PER UNIT 3
FRESH PRODUCE								
Yellow onions	$12.75	50 pound bag						
Green onions	$10.62	2 pound case						
Celery	$10.45	6 count case						
Carrots	$18.82	50 pound bag						
Apples	$30.67	72 count case						
DISPOSABLES								
Soufflé cups, 4 ounce	$49.65	2500 / case						
Souffle cup lid	$47.88	2500/ case						
Plastic wrap, 18-inch	$20.75	2000 feet						
Foil, 18-inch	$85.00	1000 feet						
Punch cups	$16.48	1000/ case						

Notice that the different products come in various package sizes. For instance, a case of salt contains twenty-four canisters, with each one weighing twenty-six ounces; peaches are packed in #10 (large) cans, which contain 35–40 peach halves per can; and meats, such as lamb, are sold and priced merely by the pound. There will always be many different package sizes, and if you're not sure about any of them, get the information from your suppliers. They'll be more than happy to help a newcomer.

Now comes the most valuable part of the process. You're going to break down the prices for different units in order to make costing easier.

First, enter the units for each item that you think will be the most important for your costing. Refer to figure 5.4 for an example.

Figure 5.4

CATEGORY	AP COST $	AP UNIT	UNIT 1	COST PER UNIT 1	UNIT 2	COST PER UNIT 2	UNIT 3	COST PER UNIT 3
DRY INGREDIENTS								
Salt	$15.20	24/26 ounce	pound		ounce		tbsp	
White pepper	$20.12	18 ounce	ounce		tbsp		tsp	
Sugar	$29.20	50 pound bag	pound		ounce			
All-purpose flour	$10.89	50 pound bag	pound		ounce			
Bread crumbs	$22.10	20 pound case	pound		ounce			
Raisins	$52.25	12/2 pound box	box		pound		ounce	
CANNED GOODS								
Peaches, 35–40 count	$37.61	6/#10 can	can		each			
White vinegar	$16.65	4/1 gallon	cup		ounce		tbsp	
Vegetable oil	$8.74	1 gallon	cup		ounce		tbsp	
Honey	$16.85	5 pound jug	pound		ounce			
Artichoke hearts	$28.45	12/14 ounce	can		each			
Mayonnaise	$26.80	4/1 gallon	gallon		pound		cup	

CATEGORY	AP COST $	AP UNIT	UNIT 1	COST PER UNIT 1	UNIT 2	COST PER UNIT 2	UNIT 3	COST PER UNIT 3
DAIRY PRODUCTS								
Whole milk	$14.15	4/1 gallon	gallon		cup		ounce	
Chocolate milk	$13.40	4/1 gallon	gallon		cup		ounce	
Heavy cream	$3.00	1 quart	cup		ounce		tbsp	
Shredded cheddar	$11.55	5 pound bag	pound		ounce			
Large eggs	$16.50	case/15 dozen	dozen		each			
FROZEN FOOD								
Vanilla ice cream	$17.35	3 gallon	gallon		cup		half cup	
Peas	$32.40	30 pound case	pound		ounce			
French fries	$30.30	6/5 pound bag	bag		pound		ounce	
Pie shells	$31.65	case of 24	each					
MEATS								
Ground beef	$41.85	20 pound case	pound		ounce			
Eye rounds	—	12/6 pounds each	pound	2.54	ounce			
Lamb rack	—	8/2 pounds each	pound	9.445	ounce			
Pork chops, bone-in	$33.95	27/6 ounces each	each					
Bacon, 14–18 count	$35.40	15 pound case	pound		ounce		slice	

CATEGORY	AP COST $	AP UNIT	UNIT 1	COST PER UNIT 1	UNIT 2	COST PER UNIT 2	UNIT 3	COST PER UNIT 3
POULTRY								
Chicken breasts, 6 ounce	$23.70	10 pound case	pound		ounce		each	
Turkey cutlets	$60.70	40/4 ounces each	each					
Cornish hens	$86.94	case of 24	each		half			
Diced chicken	$37.60	10 pound case	pound		ounce			
SEAFOOD								
Cod fillets, 8 ounce	$53.20	10 pound case	pound		each			
Shrimp, 16–20 count	$136.90	20 pound case	pound		each			
Salmon sides	—	3/2–3 pounds each	pound	11.28	ounce			
Imitation crab	$98.99	24 pound case	pound		ounce			
FRESH PRODUCE								
Yellow onions	$12.75	50 pound bag	pound		ounce			
Green onions	$10.62	2 pound case	pound		ounce			
Celery	$10.45	6 count case	each		pound		ounce	
Carrots	$18.82	50 pound bag	pound		ounce			
Apples	$30.67	72 count case	each		pound			

CATEGORY	AP COST $	AP UNIT	UNIT 1	COST PER UNIT 1	UNIT 2	COST PER UNIT 2	UNIT 3	COST PER UNIT 3
DISPOSABLES								
Soufflé cups, 4 ounce	$49.65	2500/ case	each					
Souffle cup lid	$47.88	2500/ case	each					
Plastic wrap, 18-inch	$20.75	2000 feet	foot					
Foil, 18-inch	$85.00	1000 feet	foot					
Punch cups	$16.48	1000/ case	each					

The next step is to figure out the unit prices for each item and enter them next to the corresponding unit. Let's use salt as an example.

First, we need to calculate the prices for three different units of measure:

- Unit 1: pounds
- Unit 2: ounces
- Unit 3: tablespoons

I could have used different units, but I think the ones chosen will be the most useful. To figure out the unit cost, you first have to divide the AP cost ($15.20) by the number of AP units (24) to get the cost for one 26 ounce unit. The formula looks like this:

AP Cost divided by number of AP units = cost per AP unit

$15.20 ÷ 24 = .633 (63.3 cents per 26 ounce unit)

An AP unit of salt is twenty-six ounces, so in order to calculate the per pound price, we'll first need to find out how many pounds are in twenty-six ounces. To do this, you'll take twenty-six and divide it by sixteen (ounces in a pound). Here's the procedure:

AP unit weight divided by number of ounces per pound = number of pounds per AP unit

26 ounces ÷ 16 = 1.625

This answer shows you that there are 1.625 pounds in an AP unit. To arrive at a cost per pound, divide the cost per AP unit by the number of pounds per AP unit:

Cost per AP unit divided by number of
pounds per AP unit = cost per pound

.633 ÷ 1.625 = .389 (38.9 cents per pound)

To go even further and calculate the cost per ounce, divide the cost per pound by sixteen (ounces per pound):

Cost per pound divided by number of
ounces per pound = cost per ounce

.389 ÷ 16 = .024 (2.4 cents per ounce)

Finally, to compute the cost per tablespoon, you'll need to know the number of tablespoons in each ounce of salt. There's no formula for this, so you'll have to either look it up online or manually measure tablespoons of salt until you reach one ounce. Unfortunately for me, the Internet didn't exist when I did this calculation for the first time. I discovered through measurement that there's approximately 1½ tablespoons of salt in an ounce. Here's the calculation:

Cost per ounce divided by number of
tablespoons per ounce = cost per tablespoon

.024 ÷ 1.5 (1½) = .016 (1.6 cents per tablespoon)

You'll break down the AP unit costs for the rest of the ingredients on the chart by using similar formulas. Now that you know your weight and volume measurements inside and out, this process should go relatively quickly. As you calculate the costs for the smaller units, enter them in your chart as in figure 5.5. Notice that I've highlighted the costs for salt in the chart.

Figure 5.5

CATEGORY	AP COST $	AP UNIT	UNIT 1	COST PER UNIT 1	UNIT 2	COST PER UNIT 2	UNIT 3	COST PER UNIT 3
DRY INGREDIENTS								
Salt	$15.20	24/26 ounce	pound	.389	ounce	.024	tbsp	.016
White pepper	$20.12	18 ounce	ounce	1.117	tbsp	.558	tsp	.186
Sugar	$29.20	50 pound bag	pound	.584	ounce	.036		
All-purpose flour	$10.89	50 pound bag	pound	.217	ounce	.013		
Bread crumbs	$22.10	20 pound case	pound	1.105	ounce	.069		
Raisins	$52.25	12/2 pound box	box	4.354	pound	2.177	ounce	.136
CANNED GOODS								
Peaches, 35–40 count	$37.61	6/#10 can	can	6.268	each	.167		
White vinegar	$16.65	4/1 gallon	cup	.173	ounce	.021	tbsp	.01
Vegetable oil	$8.74	1 gallon	cup	.546	ounce	.068	tbsp	.034
Honey	$16.85	5 pound jug	pound	3.37	ounce	.21		
Artichoke hearts	$28.45	12/14 ounce	can	2.37	each	.197		
Mayonnaise	$26.80	4/1 gallon	gallon	6.70	pound	.837	cup	.418
DAIRY PRODUCTS								
Whole milk	$14.15	4/1 gallon	gallon	3.537	cup	.221	ounce	.027
Chocolate milk	$13.40	4/1 gallon	gallon	3.35	cup	.209	ounce	.026
Heavy cream	$3.00	1 quart	cup	.75	ounce	.093	tbsp	.046
Shredded cheddar	$11.55	5 pound bag	pound	2.31	ounce	.144		
Large eggs	$16.50	case/15 dozen	dozen	1.10	each	.091		

CATEGORY	AP COST $	AP UNIT	UNIT 1	COST PER UNIT 1	UNIT 2	COST PER UNIT 2	UNIT 3	COST PER UNIT 3
FROZEN FOOD								
Vanilla ice cream	$17.35	3 gallon	gallon	5.783	cup	.361	half cup	.18
Peas	$32.40	30 pound case	pound	1.08	ounce	.067		
French fries	$30.30	6/5 pound bag	bag	5.05	pound	1.01	ounce	.063
Pie shells	$31.65	case of 24	each	1.318				
MEATS								
Ground beef	$41.85	20 pound case	pound	2.092	ounce	.130		
Eye rounds	—	12/6 pounds each	pound	2.54	ounce	.158		
Lamb rack	—	8/2 pounds each	pound	9.445	ounce	.59		
Pork chops, bone-in	$33.95	27/6 ounces each	each	1.257				
Bacon, 14–18 count	$35.40	15 pound case	pound	2.36	ounce	.147	slice	.147
POULTRY								
Chicken breasts, 6 ounce	$23.70	10 pound case	pound	2.37	ounce	.148	each	.888
Turkey cutlets	$60.70	40/4 ounces each	each	1.517				
Cornish hens	$86.94	case of 24	each	3.622	half	1.811		
Diced chicken	$37.60	10 pound case	pound	3.76	ounce	.235		

CATEGORY	AP COST $	AP UNIT	UNIT 1	COST PER UNIT 1	UNIT 2	COST PER UNIT 2	UNIT 3	COST PER UNIT 3
SEAFOOD								
Cod fillets, 8 ounce	$53.20	10 pound case	pound	5.32	each	2.66		
Shrimp, 16–20 count	$136.90	20 pound case	pound	6.845	each	.38		
Salmon sides	—	3/2–3 pounds each	pound	11.28	ounce	.705		
Imitation crab	$98.99	24 pound case	pound	4.124	ounce	.257		
FRESH PRODUCE								
Yellow onions	$12.75	50 pound bag	pound	.255	ounce	.015		
Green onions	$10.62	2 pound case	pound	5.31	ounce	.331		
Celery	$10.45	6 count case	each	1.741	pound	1.39	ounce	.087
Carrots	$18.82	50 pound bag	pound	.376	ounce	.023		
Apples	$30.67	72 count case	each	.425	pound	.85		
DISPOSABLES								
Soufflé cups, 4 ounce	$49.65	2500/ case	each	.019				
Souffle cup lid	$47.88	2500/ case	each	.019				
Plastic wrap, 18-inch	$20.75	2000 feet	foot	.01				
Foil, 18-inch	$85.00	1000 feet	foot	.085				
Punch cups	$16.48	1000/ case	each	.016				

Dividing down your AP ingredient costs into smaller unit costs is vital for the accurate costing of your recipes. Some of you will be starting out as small caterers, so this arithmetic shouldn't take you much time at all. If you already have a larger business, you may need more time to figure out your costs.

Some extra weighing and measuring may be necessary for the measurements that you don't have memorized. For example, you may need to figure out how many teaspoons of white pepper are in an ounce, or weigh a bunch of celery to calculate the per-pound price. Whenever you do any of these extra calculations, write the results in the side margins next to the item so that you don't have to do it again.

I suggest that you continually update costs for items that have a large price tag or wide fluctuations in price during short periods of time. This would include meats, seafood, and other more expensive items. Keep your eyes and ears open regarding the cost of produce items, which tend to go up drastically in price because of shortages or weather problems. You don't want to start losing money just because you weren't paying attention.

The prices of many items stay relatively stable over the course of a year and don't need to be updated quite so often. These items include dry goods, such as flour; oils and shortenings; and some canned goods. Again, be aware of these costs just in case there's a sudden jump in price. At the very least, I suggest that you update the cost of these types of ingredients every six months just to stay ahead of the game.

Food Costing 202: Recipe Costing for Rich Caterers

Now it's time to use your ingredient costing chart to calculate the cost of your recipes. Proper recipe costing can be somewhat time-consuming. However, when compared with the potential dollars lost through undetected costs, it's time and money well spent. Plus, you'll sleep better at night knowing that your business is definitely making a good profit. As with the previous costing section, there are recipe costing software programs available that may speed this process up a bit. Use one if you're comfortable with it.

The first step in costing out your recipes is to find a suitable recipe costing form. Both simple and elaborate forms exist. The form you use will depend on how much information you want to include and which one is easiest to understand. You can find examples of different recipe costing forms online and in textbooks. Some people just create their own using computer spreadsheets. For our exercises, we're going to use the form identified in figure 5.6.

Figure 5.6

Recipe Costing Form

Menu Item_____   Date_____

Ingredient	AP Amount	Unit	Cost per Unit	Total Ingredient Cost

Total Recipe Cost $_____
Portion Size   _____
Number of Portions   _____
Cost per Portion $_____
Cost per Ounce $_____

The next thing that we do is pick out one of our recipes for costing. For this example, let's use the carrot salad recipe we saw earlier. First, enter the recipe name and date for identification purposes. Then, enter each individual ingredient along with its AP amount and the unit used for costing. Figure 5.7 gives you an example of how everything should look.

Figure 5.7

Recipe Costing Form

Menu Item: **Carrot and Raisin Salad**   Date: **11/10/2012**

Ingredient	AP Amount	Unit	Cost per Unit	Total Ingredient Cost
Carrots, shredded	12.50 pounds	pound		
Raisins	2 pounds	pound		
Apples, chopped	4 pounds	pound		
Mayonnaise	5 cups	cup		
Salt	1 tablespoon	tablespoon		
White pepper	½ teaspoon	teaspoon		

Total Recipe Cost $_____
Portion Size   _____
Number of Portions   _____
Cost per Portion $_____
Cost per Ounce $_____

With that done, it's time to get out your ingredient costing charts. Using the charts, fill in the "Cost per Unit" column for each ingredient. See the example in figure 5.8.

Figure 5.8

Recipe Costing Form

Menu Item: **Carrot and Raisin Salad**   Date: **11/10/2012**

Ingredient	AP Amount	Unit	Cost per Unit	Total Ingredient Cost
Carrots, shredded	12.50 pounds	pound	.376	
Raisins	2 pounds	pound	2.177	
Apples, chopped	4 pounds	pound	.85	
Mayonnaise	5 cups	cup	.418	
Salt	1 tablespoon	tablespoon	.016	
White pepper	½ teaspoon	teaspoon	.186	

Total Recipe Cost $ _____
Portion Size   _____
Number of Portions   _____
Cost per Portion $ _____
Cost per Ounce $ _____

Next, for each ingredient, multiply the amount in the "AP Amount" column times the number in the "Cost per Unit" column to arrive at a total ingredient cost. Round off where necessary. I always round *up* when I do my costing, because I want the cost per portion to be a bit higher. That way, I can cover the highest possible cost when pricing my menu. Check out figure 5.9 to see how this looks.

Figure 5.9

Recipe Costing Form

Menu Item: Carrot and Raisin Salad   Date: **11/10/2012**

Ingredient	AP Amount	Unit	Cost per Unit	Total Ingredient Cost
Carrots, shredded	12.50 pounds	pound	.376	$ 4.70
Raisins	2 pounds	pound	2.177	$ 4.36
Apples, chopped	4 pounds	pound	.85	$ 3.40
Mayonnaise	5 cups	cup	.418	$ 2.09
Salt	1 tablespoon	tablespoon	.016	$.02
White pepper	½ teaspoon	teaspoon	.186	$.10

Total Recipe Cost $_____\
Portion Size   _____\
Number of Portions   _____\
Cost per Portion $_____\
Cost per Ounce $_____

Now, add up the "Total Ingredient Cost" column and enter the total on the "Total Recipe Cost" line. After that, enter the portion size and number of portions from the recipe. In this case, the portion size is four ounces and the number of portions is eighty-four. Next, divide the total recipe cost ($14.67) by the number of portions (84) and enter the amount on the "Cost per Portion" line. Finally, divide the cost per portion (.174) by the portion size (4) and enter the result on the"Cost per Ounce" line. See the illustration in figure 5.10.

Figure 5.10

Recipe Costing Form

Menu Item: **Carrot and Raisin Salad**   Date: **11/10/2012**

Ingredient	AP Amount	Unit	Cost per Unit	Total Ingredient Cost
Carrots, shredded	12.50 pounds	pound	.376	$ 4.70
Raisins	2 pounds	pound	2.177	$ 4.36
Apples, chopped	4 pounds	pound	.85	$ 3.40
Mayonnaise	5 cups	cup	.418	$ 2.09
Salt	1 tablespoon	tablespoon	.016	$.02
White pepper	½ teaspoon	teaspoon	.186	$.10

Total Recipe Cost   **$ 14.67**
Portion Size   **4 ounces**
Number of Portions   **84**
Cost per Portion   **$ .174**
Cost per Ounce   **$.044**

Most of the time, the carrot salad will be served in bowls on a buffet line. As a final exercise, let pretend that the carrot salad is going to be portioned out into 4 ounce plastic soufflé cups with lids for inclusion in a box lunch. This expense won't happen very often, but you'd like to have it handy in order to include it in the cost of the box lunch.

When you look at the ingredient costing charts, the cost for a single plastic soufflé cup is $.019 and the accompanying lid is also $.019. By adding those costs together, you'll arrive at a total of $.038 for the packaging. That's almost four cents more per portion that should be accounted for.

Since this expense is only necessary for certain items, we're going to add this entry to the last line of the recipe costing form. Then, whenever we make box lunches, the cost of the soufflé cup and lid is readily available to us. As an additional step, it's a good idea to add the extra packaging cost to the portion cost and enter the result on the form. That way, you don't need to add them up every time you prepare an item such as box lunches (see figure 5.11).

Figure 5.11

Recipe Costing Form

Menu Item: **Carrot and Raisin Salad**   Date: **11/10/2012**

Ingredient	AP Amount	Unit	Cost per Unit	Total Ingredient Cost
Carrots, shredded	12.50 pounds	pound	.376	$ 4.70
Raisins	2 pounds	pound	2.177	$ 4.36
Apples, chopped	4 pounds	pound	.85	$ 3.40
Mayonnaise	5 cups	cup	.418	$ 2.09
Salt	1 tablespoon	tablespoon	.016	$.02
White pepper	½ teaspoon	teaspoon	.186	$.10
Cost of 4 ounce soufflé cup and lid - $.038				

Box lunch:
4 oz. portion + soufflé cup and lid
.174   + .038 = .212 per portion

Total Recipe Cost	**$ 14.67**
Portion Size	**4 ounces**
Number of Portions	**84**
Cost per Portion	**$ .174**
Cost per ounce	**$.044**

What happens if you get a request for box lunches that includes a smaller size of salad, say three ounces? You have all of the information readily available to calculate the difference in cost. First, multiply the cost per ounce times three (.044 X 3 = .132). The result is the cost for a three ounce portion of carrot salad. Next, as before, enter the formula on the recipe costing form on the bottom left side as in figure 5.12.

Figure 5.12

Recipe Costing Form

Menu Item: **Carrot and Raisin Salad**   Date: **11/10/2012**

Ingredient	AP Amount	Unit	Cost per Unit	Total Ingredient Cost
Carrots, shredded	12.50 pounds	pound	.376	$ 4.70
Raisins	2 pounds	pound	2.177	$ 4.36
Apples, chopped	4 pounds	pound	.85	$ 3.40
Mayonnaise	5 cups	cup	.418	$ 2.09
Salt	1 tablespoon	tablespoon	.016	$.02
White pepper	½ teaspoon	teaspoon	.186	$.10
Cost of 4 ounce soufflé cup and lid - $.038				

Box lunch:
4 oz. portion plus soufflé cup and lid
.174 + .038 = .212 per portion
3 oz. portion plus soufflé cup and lid
.132 + .038 = .170 per portion

Total Recipe Cost	**$ 14.67**
Portion Size	**4 ounces**
Number of Portions	**84**
Cost per Portion	**$ .174**
Cost per ounce	**$.044 X 3 = .132**

Continue to modify the form as needed in order to accommodate any change in portion size or differences in packaging.

It's necessary to complete a recipe costing form such as this for each recipe you use. When you add new items to your menu, continue to cost out the recipes as you go along. When there's a large price increase for some ingredients, recalculate the cost where necessary. Then you'll always have the most current information. Make sure that the number of portions listed for each recipe is correct. Check this by dividing the total yield of the recipe by the portion size. If you're unsure what the total yield will be, prepare the recipe and carefully measure out the portions based on your desired portion size. Finally, when calculating the cost of take-out items, remember to include any packaging expense such as disposable pans, portion cups, lids, bags, foil, etc. That way, you'll be sure that all of your costs are accounted for.

There, we're finished with recipe costing. As I said before, if you had a difficult time understanding anything, go back and review it as many times as it takes until the light bulb turns on. Rich caterers know this information like the back of their hands. In time, so will you.

Pricing for Value

When a client sits down with you to plan an upcoming event, menu prices are a large part of the equation. Naturally, your client is looking for a fair price, that's a given. However, what's more important to your clients is that they feel they're getting *real value* for their money. Is there real value in spending the smallest amount of money possible for food and service? I don't think so; the cheapest prices may only buy you a less desirable experience. One of the most important things that you can do for your business is find a price point for your menu that matches the excellent food and service that you're going to deliver.

There are good and bad ways to accomplish this. Some caterers seem to enjoy picking their prices out of thin air, without rhyme or reason. It's as if they were born with all of the pricing knowledge of the universe and are *finally* able to show everyone how smart they are. People who pick prices out of the air don't really pay much attention to their costs. They're just guessing that they'll make a profit, but they don't really know. Maybe they should use their incredible insight to play the lottery instead of catering.

Other caterers know their costs, but keep their prices unusually low, because they're embarrassed about asking for more money and don't think that they deserve it. I'm no psychiatrist (thank goodness), but I think that it's really a self-esteem problem. If these people are so ashamed of what they offer, they should start a business where they don't need to charge as much money for their service, perhaps as a dog walker.

Then there are the caterers who ignore their costs and set their prices way above the market. These wisenheimers are positive that they're just going to make a killing in catering. Typically, these folks have had very limited experience in the food service industry. They may have been employed as bartenders, cooks, or servers at one time or another and are convinced that they know more than everyone else. They don't. They'll be shocked when potential clients go somewhere else in order to get more value for their dollar. Instead of making a killing, they end up being the victim.

The prices on your menu are going to affect the future balance in your bank account and your eventual retirement. Let's face it: besides your health and family, there isn't much that's more important. You should approach menu pricing with a clear head, a lot of information, and a big dose of common sense.

So, where do you start? A good rule of thumb when pricing your menu is to make sure that the cost of each menu item is about 25 percent of its selling price. That means if the ingredients for an item cost $1.00, you should sell that item for about $4.00. That seems simple enough, but some items could be sold for much more money because of their popularity or demand. In this case, you should sell them for as much as possible without affecting sales. On the other hand, some menu items may contain seafood or other expensive ingredients that would be a bit too pricey using the above-mentioned 25 percent rule. When that happens, set the price as low as possible, while still making a decent profit. If the cost is too prohibitive, you might have to drop the item from your menu altogether.

At this point you should be asking yourself, "Isn't there a way to price my menu which factors in all of these variables?" Yes there is, and it will even include your target market. A potential rich caterer (such as yourself) should use all of the information available instead of trying to reinvent the wheel.

Remember those sample menus and catering packets that you collected from every caterer in your area? We'll be able to use them once again to get information for pricing your menu. Usually your direct competitors have a pretty good idea of where their prices should be, especially if they've been in business a long time.

The first thing that you'll need to do is find information from the caterers who are most like you. Search out caterers whose menus and service styles are similar to yours. The more information you can get from them, the better. Next, look at your menu and compare it to your competition. Seek out similar menu items and write down the competitor's prices. There will always be items on your menu that have no comparison, but at least you'll have a starting point. No doubt your competitors have been working on their prices for many years, so the prices they charge should match well with your target market. Once you've done all of your research, you should see a definite price *range* for your menu.

The next step is to assign *specific* prices to your menu. This is decision time, so think about this carefully. Will you try to undercut your competition a little bit and possibly draw in more customers? Maybe you want your prices somewhere in the middle, thinking that you don't want to rock the boat with prices that are too high. You could also set your prices on the upper end of the market, using the value of your catering style to make more money. Let's discuss each of these options.

On the low end, you're thinking that lower prices will draw in more customers. This isn't necessarily so. Remember, you're a wow-factor caterer. It won't be your prices that attract potential clients, it will be the *real value* you provide for the money. Your clients are going to receive superior quality food and excellent service. Do you really want to work the same number of hours and spend the same amount of money to execute a fabulous function and get paid *less* for it? I'd stay away from this low price idea if you truly want to make some money. Rich caterers are proud of the fantastic food and service that they offer and aren't afraid to charge more for it.

How about charging what everyone else charges? That would be a great idea…if everyone else was a wow-factor caterer, like you. However, you and I both know that the food and service you'll offer will be much better than most of your competition. So pricing your menu like everyone else will be like giving out the extra service you provide for *free*. Your clients will love it, and you might make some money, but you'll have to work longer and harder to earn it. If you're like me, you'll want to maximize your profits and build up that retirement account as quickly as possible. This might not be the best way to do it.

Before we discuss the last option, you and I are going to have a little heart-to-heart chat. The goal that you've set for yourself and your business is to become a rich caterer. Some of you may have a difficult time following through on that. Maybe it's because your father taught you that money is bad and every rich person is a crook. Perhaps your mission in life is to make people happy, and charging them less keeps everyone smiling. Or it could be that you just hate confrontation, and if you charge people more money, they might get mad at you and start throwing punches. If you find yourself in these descriptions, perhaps you should consider talking to a therapist *first,* before further pursuing a career in catering.

For the rest of you, I think this is the right time to do an exercise that I like to call, "The Rich Caterer's Reflection." Please go to the nearest mirror—the bathroom mirror is fine. Stand tall, look yourself in the eye, and confidently recite the following "Rich Caterer's Credo" to the person in the mirror:

> **"I'm a rich caterer, and I charge more**
> **because it's *worth* more."**

You may have felt a little strange about talking to yourself in a mirror, but I hope you felt good about the credo. If you didn't, repeat it again but with more feeling. In fact, keep repeating it until you realize, as I do, that catering is hard work, and you deserve to make a fair profit. I want you to understand something. Your business will create some extraordinary events that are going to influence people's lives for the better. For providing that service, you have every right to charge a little more.

Now, let's return to menu-pricing options. Your last and best option is to price your menu along with the top 5 percent of the other caterers in the area. They are (or should be) offering excellent food and service, and you deserve to be grouped with them. When prospective clients are looking for a really incredible catering experience, you want to be on the short list of caterers ready to serve them. You charge more, because you're worth it. Never forget that or apologize for it.

How much should you charge? Only you can answer that. The same menu in different locations will be priced differently. The prices on a menu in a predominantly rural area will be completely different from the same menu in New York City. Use all of the information that you have available, and make your decisions based on that. Use the 25 percent rule wherever possible, and always check your costs to be sure that you're making a good buck. If you make a mistake and realize that you're charging too much or too little for something, change it as soon as possible. Your menu and its pricing will always be a work in progress. You will continue to add new items and remove others. As long as you keep your costing information up to date, and change your prices when necessary, everything will be just fine.

THE BOOK OF
PROFITABLE PORTIONS
Cleverly Controlling Food Quantities

Size Does Matter

So far, you've done some incredible work. However, all of this preparation won't do you any good, if you lose money by portioning food improperly. Correct portioning is the only way to insure that you'll be preparing the right amount of food for your guests with very little waste. This is actually an easy process that uses some basic rules of thumb and common sense. Luckily, many caterers before you have come up with these rules, and they work pretty well. Here's a list of some general portion sizes for various food categories:

Food Category	Plated Meal	Buffet
Main entrées (cooked weight)	5–6 ounces	4 ounces
Gravy or sauce	2 ounces	3 ounces
Cooked vegetables	4 ounces	3 ounces
Starch (potatoes, rice, pasta, etc.)	4 ounces	3 ounces
Bound salads (potato, macaroni, etc.)	4 ounces	3 ounces
Green salads	3–4 ounces	3 ounces
Fruit salads	4 ounces	3 ounces
Soup (cup)	6 ounces	6 ounces

Why the difference in portion sizes between plated meals and buffets? It starts with the plate size. Dinner plates for served meals are generally larger. That way, the food doesn't look crowded on the plate, and it has a more pleasing appearance to the guest. The amount of food on the plate is completely controlled by you and your staff, so there will be no over-portioning.

On the other hand, buffet diners can eat as much food as they want. You can't control how much they take. The phrase "your eyes are bigger than your stomach" comes into play here. So, you certainly don't want your ravenously hungry guests to pile up that delicious food on a *large* plate and leave half of it there to be thrown away later. That would be a horrible waste of food and money. Rich caterers are smarter than that. They use smaller plates, maybe eight and a half to nine inches in diameter in order to discourage overfilling. If your guests want more after the first plate, they can certainly go back and fill up another plate (we will discuss charging by the plate in a later chapter).

You might have noticed that the amount of sauce per guest actually gets *larger* on a buffet. This isn't because your diners eat more sauce on a buffet...they don't. However, because meats on a buffet are set up in metal pans, it takes a little more sauce to cover the meat and fill up the empty spaces around it to make the meat look more appealing. Our goal is to serve fabulous food. A pan of meat that's covered by just a tiny amount of sauce looks dry and not very pleasing.

The portion sizes for the different food categories are approximates and will vary depending on the specific type of food that you're using, the number of items on the buffet, and your clientele. Nothing is ever set in stone. As a soon-to-be rich caterer, you should continue to gather portion size information and use it to your advantage as your business grows.

Now that you know the approximate portion sizes, I'm going to let you in on a little portioning secret:

Smaller Pieces = Bigger Profits

Let me illustrate this point for you. Imagine that you're going to prepare roast beef for a buffet. According to the portioning chart, you decide to serve a four-ounce portion of meat to each guest. You have your staff slice the roast beef into single four-ounce slices, so that each guest will get one slice per portion. You line up the slices neatly in the metal pan, cover the beef with gravy, and heat it to serving temperature. At service time, you put the roast beef in the chafing dish and watch as the guests go through the buffet. Your first guest takes one slice of beef and moves on. The second guest wants more than four ounces and takes two slices (a double portion). The third guest doesn't normally eat much beef, but would just like a taste. In order to get a smaller piece, guest number three tries to tear a piece in half, right in the chafing dish. After several tries, this guest relents to the pressure of holding up the line and decides to just take a whole piece and eat only half of it. Now let's tally up the amount of beef used by these three guests.

Guest 1: 4 ounces
Guest 2: 8 ounces
Guest 3: 4 ounces
Total: 16 ounces beef ÷ 3 guests = 5.33 ounces per person

By giving the guests only one slice per portion, you have unknowingly caused over-portioning problems. Let's try this again and do it more efficiently.

Imagine that you're going to prepare roast beef for a buffet. According to the portioning chart, you decide to serve four ounces of meat to each guest. You have your staff slice the roast beef into four-ounce slices and then cut the slices *in half*, so that each guest will get *two-two-ounce slices* per portion. Continue on as before. When the guests start coming through the buffet, you'll notice something different this time. Your first guest takes two slices of beef (four ounces) and moves on. The second guest wants more than four ounces and takes three slices (a six-ounce portion). The third guest doesn't normally eat much beef but would like a taste and takes just one slice (two ounces). Again, let's add the amount of beef used by these three guests.

Guest 1: 4 ounces
Guest 2: 6 ounces
Guest 3: 2 ounces
Total: 12 ounces beef ÷ 3 guests = 4 ounces per person

As you can see, cutting the beef into smaller slices kept the portions right on target. You have used less meat and generated more money for your business in the process. This is just an example, but as a general rule, when food is cut into smaller pieces, people will put less on their plates. Less food consumption means more money for you—it's a fact!

This secret works great for many other items as well. Vegetable and fruit displays are a good example. If you would normally cut the fruit or vegetables into larger chunks, try cutting them into pieces that are three-fourths or even half the size you normally would. This creates more space between the pieces, and the same amount of fruit will appear to have grown in volume. Four ounces of smaller-cut fruit or vegetables will *look* like a larger portion, and guests will take less when going through the buffet line. Once again, you've used less product and generated extra income.

Cheese trays are another good example. You can do it yourself if you don't believe me. Slice one pound of cheddar cheese into quarter-inch thick slices, approximately one inch wide and two inches long (cracker size). Arrange the cheese nicely on a small platter. Next, slice another pound of cheddar, only this time make the slices an eighth of an inch thick. Arrange these *thinner* slices on a similar small platter. The second pile of cheese looks bigger, doesn't it? That's because there are more slices and more spaces between them. At this point you may be thinking that you could make your cheese trays with a little less cheese and still have them *look* like they contain the same amount. *Bingo!* Now you're starting to think like a rich caterer. Meat trays, sausage trays, seafood trays, dessert trays—they all work the same way.

So remember this simple rule for cutting and portioning food: If you want to make BIG money…think small.

Cash in the Trash

Preparing too much food for a catered event is just like throwing money in the trash. Overproduction usually means that at least some food will end up in the garbage can. And even if it doesn't, extra food means extra production time, extra cooling time, extra packaging, and extra storage time. Time is definitely money, my friends. Think of all that expense, without any guarantee that you can recover your losses. That's why being as perfect as possible when calculating food quantities for an event is so important.

The amount of food you prepare for any given event is based primarily on the portion size, the number of people attending, and the percentage of people who'll eat each individual item. Let me explain how this works. Let's say that you're preparing the following menu for one hundred people:

- Chicken noodle soup
- Swiss steaks with gravy
- Mashed potatoes
- Green beans almandine
- Caramel apple pie

Scenario #1: A Plated Meal
If this menu is plated and served to guests in the dining room, calculating how much to prepare will be somewhat simple, since each guest will be given some of everything on the menu.

Let's begin with the chicken noodle soup. The portion size is six volume ounces, and if everyone receives one portion, the total amount of soup would be six hundred ounces (six ounces x one hundred guests). From experience, I know that there are 128 volume ounces in a gallon. So, I take the total ounces and divide it by the number of ounces in a gallon to find out how many gallons of soup to make. It should appear this way:

Total ounces divided by number of ounces
per gallon = number of gallons needed

600 ounces ÷ 128 ounces in a gallon = 4.6875 gallons

If you know that you need 4.6875 gallons of soup, convert your recipe so that it makes a little more than that, somewhere between 4.75 and 5 gallons. That way, if someone asks for an extra cup, or your server, Butterfinger Bert, drops one on the way to the dining room, you've covered yourself.

Now let's repeat this process for the Swiss Steaks. Each guest will be served one six-ounce portion (cooked weight). Again, multiply six ounces (weight) by one hundred guests, which totals six hundred ounces. Since these are weight ounces, the calculation will be a little different:

Total ounces divided by number of ounces
per pound = number of pounds needed

600 ounces ÷ 16 ounces per pound =
37.50 pounds of Swiss Steak meat

Since this is cooked weight and not raw weight, you'll have to finish your calculations by dividing the cooked weight by the yield percentage. If you're not sure how to do this, refer back to the section on shrinkage in "The Book of Maximum Yields." For our example, let's figure a yield percentage of 66 percent. The formula should look like this:

Final cooked weight divided by yield percentage = AP weight

37.50 pounds ÷ 66% (.66) = 57 pounds (56.81)

Make sure that you purchase a little bit more meat, perhaps sixty pounds, in case of mishaps.

For the gravy, the portion is two ounces, so that means you'll need two hundred volume ounces. As before, divide the total by 128 to arrive at the number of gallons to prepare:

Total ounces divided by number of ounces
per gallon = number of gallons needed

200 ounces ÷ 128 ounces in a gallon = 1.56 gallons
Convert your recipe to make about 1.75 gallons, just to be safe.

The potatoes and beans have the exact same equations:

100 guests x 4 ounce (weight) portion per guest = 400
400 ounces ÷ 16 ounces per pound = 25 pounds

You'll need to convert your recipes to produce a little over twenty-five pounds of each item, and don't forget to follow your AP and EP percentages when converting.

Finally, you have the caramel apple pie. The portion is one piece per person, but the size of the piece depends on the size of the pie. Is it an eight-, nine-, or ten-inch pie? Once you figure that out, you can calculate the number of pieces. How big should you cut the pieces? Consider that your guests have already eaten a full meal. I think that you should always serve the *smallest acceptable* piece of dessert. That doesn't mean that you cut the pie into twenty pieces (too small); nor should you cut it into six pieces (way too big). Try to make it somewhere in between. The size of the dessert you serve at that point should be enough to give your guests a taste of something sweet but not so much that they're overstuffed. For this scenario, let's say we're cutting a ten-inch pie into twelve pieces. You'll need one piece for each guest, so that's one hundred total pieces of pie. The next calculation is:

100 total pieces ÷ 12 slices per pie = 8.33 pies

Of course you can't make 8.33 pies, so you'll have to make at least nine, possibly ten, just in case someone trips and drops a whole pie on the floor (it happens).

Scenario #2: A Buffet

If this menu is being set up as a buffet, the amounts you prepare will be a bit different, since your guests can have as much or as little as they want. What you have to do is figure out how many people will be eating each item on the menu.

We'll start again with the chicken noodle soup. The calculation we used for the plated meal would be correct if *everyone* going through the buffet line were eating soup. The fact is, that's just not going to happen. There will always be some people who don't like chicken noodle soup or simply don't want to eat soup that day. So, how many people will eat soup? Consumption depends on the type of soup, the temperature outside, your geographic location, and other factors. A good rule of thumb would be 75–80 percent of the group. Figuring on the high side, let's say that 80 percent (80 people) will eat chicken noodle soup at the event. Here are the formulas:

$$80 \text{ guests} \times 6 \text{ ounces} = 480 \text{ total ounces}$$

$$480 \text{ total ounces} \div 128 \text{ ounces in a gallon} = 3.75 \text{ gallons}$$

As you can see, you need much less soup for a buffet than for a plated meal.

When you first start figuring out your food production amounts, you might want to go even a little higher on your percentage to cover yourself, in case a larger number of people eat soup than expected. As you become more experienced with your menu and familiar with your clientele, your chances of overproduction will diminish. Now let's calculate the amounts for the rest of the items on the menu.

The number of Swiss steaks you'll need for a buffet will be higher because some people will take two of them. You can offset that extra expense by cutting the meat into smaller steaks, perhaps four ounces (cooked weight). Remember, smaller pieces are more profitable. After filling their plates up with everything else, I estimate that most guests will take one steak. Some will take two, and the average serving per guest will be about six ounces. Again, that's six ounces (weight) multiplied by one hundred guests, which is six hundred ounces. Don't forget, these are weight ounces, so the equation will look like this:

Total ounces divided by number of ounces
per pound = number of pounds needed

600 ounces ÷ 16 ounces
per pound = 37.50 pounds of Swiss Steak meat

Once again, you'll have to finish your calculations by dividing the cooked weight by the yield percentage. Since it's the same amount of meat as the plated meal, the calculation is identical:

Final cooked weight divided by yield percentage = AP weight

37.50 pounds ÷ 66% (.66) = 57 pounds (56.81)

As before, make sure to purchase a little extra meat to compensate for Butterfinger Bert.

The amount of gravy required for a buffet is different, since the chafing dish needs to look full. The gravy portion per serving is three ounces, so that means you'll need three hundred volume ounces. As before, divide the total by 128 to arrive at the amount of gallons to prepare:

Total ounces divided by number of
ounces per gallon = number of gallons needed

300 ounces ÷ 128 ounces in a gallon = 2.34 gallons

Convert your recipe to make about 2.50 gallons for safety's sake.

You'll be preparing fewer potatoes and beans for a buffet, because the portion is smaller. Use the same formulas as before:

100 guests x three ounces (weight) portion per guest = 300
300 ounces ÷ 16 ounces per pound = 18.75 pounds

You'll need to convert your recipes to produce a little over 18.75 pounds of each item, and again, don't forget to follow your AP and EP percentages when converting.

Once again, our final item is the caramel apple pie. The theory here is the same as for the Swiss steak. Some people won't take any, and some will take two pieces. We should still estimate one slice per person and use the same size that we did for the plated meal. Since we've already done the calculations for that, there's no need to do them again. Make nine or ten pies at your discretion.

Well, that's how you calculate portions and food production in a nutshell. When you begin your business, it won't be an exact science. As I mentioned before, many factors will affect how much food you'll need to produce and serve. Continually observe and record any changes in consumption over time. Discuss food production quantities with your staff, and then tweak the numbers until you get as close as humanly possible to exact amounts. Even after you think that everything is under control, continue to monitor portions and production at every event, just in case the percentage changes drastically one way or the other. Rich caterers do this, because they know that over-producing food is like throwing cash in the trash.

Counting Is Critical

A rich caterer tends to have a generous amount of well-placed obsessive compulsiveness when it comes to counting. I'm not talking about pushing the correct buttons on the calculator. I hope you can do that without my input. I'm also pretty sure that you can count *without* a calculator. No problem there. What's truly critical is the ability to count at the proper time, in the right way, at multiple points, and with accuracy. Consider the following.

Situation A

You're serving a wedding for five hundred guests. You've ordered one dinner roll per person from the local bakery, and they were delivered to your establishment at noon. You assign someone from your early shift (Pam) to put them on large pans and store them in the kitchen for safe keeping until service time at 6:30 p.m. Just before service, you have another staff member (Jake) transfer the rolls to smaller serving trays. You decide to set one tray out on the serving line at a time, as needed. After approximately four hundred guests have been through the buffet, you notice that there are no serving trays of rolls left in the kitchen, and just a few rolls out on the serving line. In one minute, hungry diners are going to ask you for more rolls, and you don't have any. What do you do now? Well, hopefully the supermarket is open and they have an acceptable type of dinner roll. You'll have to send one of your staff there with a fistful of cash to purchase more. Meanwhile, you'll be apologizing profusely to annoyed guests, promising to bring them fresh rolls as soon as they arrive (if ever). All the while, you'll be wondering what got you into this mess. The answer is simple arithmetic. When the rolls were delivered, you didn't count them to confirm that the order was correct. Lots of bad things can happen if you don't count deliveries to make sure that they're accurate. If you would have counted the rolls at delivery time, you'd have known that the order was short and could have called the bakery for the rest of the order. If they didn't have any more rolls, then you could have gone to the supermarket a few hours before service time and easily picked up something acceptable with plenty of time to spare. In this situation, you let something as simple as counting a delivery foul up your event.

Situation B

You're serving a wedding for five hundred guests. You've ordered one dinner roll per person from the local bakery, and they were delivered to your establishment at noon. You *count* them to make sure that your order is correct and find that there are exactly five hundred dinner rolls. You assign Pam to put the rolls on large pans and store them back in the kitchen until service time. She sees a storage cabinet with a few slots available and starts sliding the pans in. When she gets to the last pan of rolls, Pam discovers that there's no more space left in the cabinet. She decides it's a good idea to put the the rolls *on top* of the cabinet instead. The pan is a little hard to see, but she'll remember where it is. Just before service, you have Jake transfer the rolls to smaller serving trays as before. After approximately four hundred guests have gone through the buffet, you notice that there are no serving trays left in the kitchen and just a few rolls out on the serving line. How can this be? You know that there were five hundred rolls, because you counted them. You want to ask Pam where the remaining rolls are, but she worked the early shift and you sent her home ten minutes ago. *Oops!* She forgot to tell you about the hidden rolls on top of the cabinet. You call her cell phone, but she won't answer while she's driving. You messed up again! You need to do something *fast*, so out goes another staff member to the supermarket with another fistful of money. The week after the fiasco, you discover the dried out dinner rolls on top of the cabinet in the kitchen. You think back to the angry guests and realize that it all could have been avoided. Let's do it the right way this time—the rich caterer's way.

Situation C

You're serving a wedding for five hundred guests. You've ordered one dinner roll per person from the local bakery, and they were delivered to your establishment at noon. You count them *once* to make sure that there are exactly five hundred dinner rolls. You assign Pam to put the rolls on large pans and store them back in the kitchen until service time. You've instructed Pam to count them a *second* time and *put one hundred rolls on each pan so that they can easily be recounted later.* She sees a storage cabinet with a few slots available and starts sliding the pans in. When she gets to the last pan of rolls, Pam discovers that there's no more space left in the cabinet. She decides it's a good idea to put the the rolls *on top* of the cabinet instead. The pan is a little hard to see, but she'll remember where it is. Before Jake transfers the rolls to smaller serving trays, you ask him to count the rolls a *third* time and make sure that there are five hundred total. From previous catering events, Jake knows that there are one hundred dinner rolls on each pan, so he just counts the pans in the cabinet and comes up with four—that's only four hundred rolls. Jake tells you about the problem, and you ask Pam where the other rolls are. She remembers that there's one pan on top of the cabinet and points it out to Jake. Jake then arranges the dinner rolls on the serving trays. The buffet goes off without a hitch. After the last of the guests comes through the buffet line, the mother of the bride walks up to you and says what a wonderful job you've done and that everything was perfect. She's right, too; there was no anger, no drama, and no extra outlay of cash to the supermarket. Well done, rich caterer!

THE BOOK OF
SAVVY PURCHASING
How to Get More for Less

Pretend It's Your New Car

Let's imagine that you're going to purchase a new car. You've already selected the model that you want and proceed to visit the nearest car dealership to take a test drive. After a few spins around the neighborhood, you decide that your selected vehicle is perfect for you. You tell the sales associate about your decision, and he directs your attention to the car's *sticker price* for your consideration. You agree that the sticker price is indeed fair and proceed to the office to sign the paperwork. You emerge from the office as the proud owner of a fabulous new car. As you drive away, you smile broadly and marvel at how easy the whole process was.

Right about now, you're probably shaking your head and thinking, "That's not how the car-buying process really works," and you'd be right. If you're like most people, looking for a new car involves trying to get a good deal on the vehicle. You want to pay less than the sticker price so that your new car has more *value* for each dollar you spend.

But getting a good deal takes a little bit of work, doesn't it? So you do some research about how much money the car is actually worth. You find out what other customers have paid for the exact same model. Maybe you'll go online and ask other buyers about their satisfaction with the car. Perhaps you'll surf around a few car evaluation websites to see what independent evaluators think of your chosen car and what the value is. When you're done investigating, you feel pretty confident about your ability to get a good deal. One thing is for sure: *you're not going to pay one penny more than necessary to purchase that car!*

When you visit the dealerships (more than one, of course), you come prepared with all of the facts and figures that you'll need in order to negotiate what you consider to be a good price for the car. You're prepared to haggle with the sales people or maybe even walk out the door in order to show that you're serious about getting a fair price. When you finally sign the papers, you know that you did everything possible in order to pay the least amount necessary for your new car.

Food ordering is no different. You'll spend thousands of dollars every week to purchase food for your various catered events. When ordering food for your business, paying the lowest price for raw materials is crucial to your bottom line. In order to be a savvy purchaser, you'll have to put forth some extra time and effort with research, just as you did with getting a good deal on a new car. The process is similar and much more rewarding.

Rich caterers know that poor food ordering skills and poor profits go hand-in-hand. Therefore…

Using proper food ordering techniques is the fourth *nonnegotiable, absolutely essential* **part of running a catering business that attracts big money.**

Ordering Food Intelligently

You need to be smart when you order food for your business. The food ordering process itself is basically very simple, but, as with any critical area of catering, attention to detail will make the difference between earning an average amount of money and becoming a rich caterer.

First, contact all of the local food suppliers that deliver to your area. Ask each food supplier for the name of a sales representative who will handle your account and request that he or she call you personally to set up an appointment to review prices. You may know some of these people already from previous experience.

Once you've gotten the appointments booked, you're ready for step two. Remember the costing charts you created that included all of your recipe ingredients? They're going to come in handy now, as a homework assignment for the supplier sales reps you're meeting with. You'll need to modify the form slightly for this purpose. Since you probably have the form saved on a computer, it'll only take a little revision to make it work. You've already included the AP units for each item, so that'll make it easier. Change the column headings so that they match the ones in figure 7.1.

Figure 7.1

CATEGORY	AP UNIT	VENDOR 1	VENDOR 2	VENDOR 3	VENDOR 4
DRY INGREDIENTS					
Salt	24/26 ounces				
White pepper	18 ounce				
Sugar	50 pound bag				
All-purpose flour	50 pound bag				
Bread crumbs	20 pound case				
Raisins	12/2 pound box				
CANNED GOODS					
Peaches, 35–40 count	6/#10 can				
White vinegar	4/1 gallon				
Vegetable oil	1 gallon				
Honey	5 pound jug				
Artichoke hearts	12/14 ounce				
Mayonnaise	4/1 gallon				
DAIRY PRODUCTS					
Whole milk	4/1 gallon				
Chocolate milk	4/1 gallon				
Heavy cream	1 quart				
Shredded cheddar	5 pound bag				
Large eggs	case/15 dozen				
FROZEN FOOD					
Vanilla ice cream	3 gallon				
Peas	30 pound case				
French fries	6/5 pound bag				
Pie shells	case of 24				

CATEGORY	AP UNIT	VENDOR 1	VENDOR 2	VENDOR 3	VENDOR 4
MEATS					
Ground beef	20 pound case				
Eye rounds	12/6 pounds each				
Lamb rack	8/2 pounds each				
Pork chops, bone-in	27/6 ounces each				
Bacon, 14–18 count	15 pound case				
POULTRY					
Chicken breasts, 6 ounce	10 pound case				
Turkey cutlets	40/4 ounces each				
Cornish hens	case of 24				
Diced chicken	10 pound case				
SEAFOOD					
Cod fillets, 8 ounce	10 pound case				
Shrimp, 16–20 count	20 pound case				
Salmon sides	3/2–3 pounds each				
Imitation crab	24 pound case				
FRESH PRODUCE					
Yellow onions	50 pound bag				
Green onions	2 pound case				
Celery	6 count case				
Carrots	50 pound bag				
Apples	72 count case				

CATEGORY	AP UNIT	VENDOR 1	VENDOR 2	VENDOR 3	VENDOR 4
DISPOSABLES					
Soufflé cups, 4 ounce	2500/case				
Souffle cup lid	2500/case				
Plastic wrap, 18-inch	2000 feet				
Foil, 18-inch	1000 feet				
Punch cups	1000/case				

Notice I've changed the column headings to accommodate the names of your vendors. I also modified the AP unit column for each of the meat items to read their specific pack size. This will make it easier for the vendors to quote a price per pound.

When the form is finished, print out as many blank costing lists as you have appointments with vendors, and then maybe a couple of extra copies for you to use later. When you meet with them, hand each sales representative a copy of your list and explain that you'd like a price quote for each of the items listed. Some of the companies you meet with might only deal in certain types of products, such as dairy, meat, or produce. That's fine; just ask them to fill out the part of the list that includes those items. However, it is crucial that you have at least two vendors who are able to supply most of the items you'll need on a regular basis. This will create the competitive atmosphere you'll need in order to receive the lowest prices on most items. Ask each sales representative to take the list and return it to you in a week or two. Set a follow-up meeting and wave good-bye.

At this point, I must tell you that some of the representatives won't take this task as seriously as you do. They'll come back to the next meeting and have excuses about why they couldn't complete your list, or only partially complete it. That's okay - just take what they give you and thank them for their precious time. When all of the vendor's price lists are in, you can move on to the next step.

Now we're going to assemble the current prices into a form that you may use to compare them. Take out the extra blank costing sheets that you printed and write the names of your suppliers on the top, as in figure 7.2. If you discover that you need more columns, modify the list on your computer by adding the number of columns necessary for this task and continue.

Figure 7.2

CATEGORY	AP UNIT	VENDOR 1 US SUPPLY	VENDOR 2 ZZZ FOODS	VENDOR 3 HOME DAIRY	VENDOR 4 A-1 PRODUCE
DRY INGREDIENTS					
Salt	24/26 ounces				
White pepper	18 ounces				
Sugar	50 pound bag				
All-purpose flour	50 pound bag				
Bread crumbs	20 pound case				
Raisins	12/2 pound box				

Once you've written in the vendors, you can add their price quotes to the form for comparison. For our purposes, we'll start with vendor #1, US Supply, and insert their prices for each item on the form in figure 7.3:

Figure 7.3

CATEGORY	AP UNIT	VENDOR 1 US SUPPLY	VENDOR 2 ZZZ FOODS	VENDOR 3 HOME DAIRY	VENDOR 4 A-1 PRODUCE
DRY INGREDIENTS					
Salt	24/26 ounce	19.58			
White pepper	18 ounce	19.98			
Sugar	50 pound bag	48.66			
All-purpose flour	50 pound bag	18.14			
Bread crumbs	20 pound case	24.92			
Raisins	12/2 pound box	59.39 (30#)			
CANNED GOODS					
Peaches, 35–40 count	6/#10 can	33.74			
White vinegar	4/1 gallon	13.79			
Vegetable oil	1 gallon	8.63			
Honey	5 pound jug	16.51			
Artichoke hearts	12/14 ounce	—			
Mayonnaise	4/1 gallon	33.40			

CATEGORY	AP UNIT	VENDOR 1 US SUPPLY	VENDOR 2 ZZZ FOODS	VENDOR 3 HOME DAIRY	VENDOR 4 A-1 PRODUCE
DAIRY PRODUCTS					
Whole milk	4/1 gallon	16.85			
Chocolate milk	4/1 gallon	15.08			
Heavy cream	1 quart	6.44 (1/2 gal.)			
Shredded cheddar	5 pound bag	12.61			
Large eggs	case/15 dozen	18.27			
FROZEN FOOD					
Vanilla ice cream	3 gallon	14.19			
Peas	30 pound case	24.68 (20#)			
French fries	6/5 pound bag	26.03			
Pie shells	case of 24	31.94			
MEATS					
Ground beef	20 pound case	45.90			
Eye rounds	12/6 pounds each	2.42/ pound			
Lamb rack	8/2 pounds each	10.50/ pound			
Pork chops, bone-in	27/6 ounces each	34.61/ case			
Bacon, 14–18 count	15 pound case	31.98			
POULTRY					
Chicken breasts, 6 ounce	10 pound case	35.00 (20 #)			
Turkey cutlets	40/4 ounces each	61.02			
Cornish hens	case of 24	43.38 (1/2s)			
Diced chicken	10 pound case	29.46			

CATEGORY	AP UNIT	VENDOR 1 US SUPPLY	VENDOR 2 ZZZ FOODS	VENDOR 3 HOME DAIRY	VENDOR 4 A-1 PRODUCE
SEAFOOD					
Cod fillets, 8 ounce	10 pound case	60.96			
Shrimp, 16–20 count	20 pound case	149.08			
Salmon sides	3/2–3 pounds each	11.52/ pound			
Imitation crab	24 pound case	33.44 (10#)			
FRESH PRODUCE					
Yellow onions	50 pound bag	14.66			
Green onions	2 pound case	5.43			
Celery	6 count case	14.53			
Carrots	50 pound bag	34.29			
Apples	72 count case	50.51			
DISPOSABLES					
Soufflé cups, 4 ounce	2500/case	49.65			
Souffle cup lid	2500/case	47.88			
Plastic wrap, 18-inch	2000 feet	22.75			
Foil, 18-inch	1000 feet	45.26			
Punch cups	1000/case	63.68			

As you enter prices for US Supply, a few things become apparent:

- Under "Dry Ingredients," the company has quoted the raisins price for a thirty-pound case. You may have to break this down further later, but for now, just enter the price and make a notation for 30# (pounds).
- In the "Canned Goods" section, US Supply doesn't carry artichoke hearts in small cans, and you don't want the large cans, so just put a line through it and move on.
- In the "Dairy Products" section, the vendor only offers heavy cream in a half-gallon size. A change of the unit price may be needed to compare it to other suppliers properly. Enter the price and make the notation "1/2 gal."
- In the "Frozen Food" section, US Supply only offers frozen peas in a twenty-pound case. It may be necessary to

convert this to a price per pound for comparison. For the moment, enter the price and make the notation for 20#.

- Under "Poultry," the company has quoted the chicken breast price for a twenty-pound case. Make the notation and continue.
- In the same category, US Supply only offers Cornish hen *halves*, not the whole bird. This may not work for your menu, but you make the notation "1/2s" just in case.
- Under "Seafood," the imitation crab is only quoted for a ten-pound case. Most likely, you'll need to break this price down later for a per pound price comparison. For now, simply make the notation.

All of the other price quotes from US Supply are correct for the pack size, and we can now enter the prices for ZZZ Foods in the form, as shown in figure 7.4.

Figure 7.4

CATEGORY	AP UNIT	VENDOR 1 US SUPPLY	VENDOR 2 ZZZ FOODS	VENDOR 3 HOME DAIRY	VENDOR 4 A-1 PRODUCE
DRY INGREDIENTS					
Salt	24/26 ounce	19.58	20.02		
White pepper	18 ounce	19.98	23.10		
Sugar	50 pound bag	48.66	49.20		
All-purpose flour	50 pound bag	18.14	19.00		
Bread crumbs	20 pound case	24.92	25.25		
Raisins	12/2 pound box	59.39 (30#)	52.33		
CANNED GOODS					
Peaches, 35–40 count	6/#10 can	33.74	32.97		
White vinegar	4/1 gallon	13.79	14.87		
Vegetable oil	1 gallon	8.63	9.55		
Honey	5 pound jug	16.51	15.99		
Artichoke hearts	12/14 ounce	—	24.43		
Mayonnaise	4/1 gallon	33.40	36.64		

CATEGORY	AP UNIT	VENDOR 1 US SUPPLY	VENDOR 2 ZZZ FOODS	VENDOR 3 HOME DAIRY	VENDOR 4 A-1 PRODUCE
DAIRY PRODUCTS					
Whole milk	4/1 gallon	16.85	17.05		
Chocolate milk	4/1 gallon	15.08	16.20		
Heavy cream	1 quart	6.44 (1/2 gal.)	3.56		
Shredded cheddar	5 pound bag	12.61	12.88		
Large eggs	case/15 dozen	18.27	19.12		
FROZEN FOOD					
Vanilla ice cream	3 gallon	14.19	17.99		
Peas	30 pound case	24.68 (20#)	45.00		
French fries	6/5 pound bag	26.03	28.28		
Pie shells	case of 24	31.94	36.78		
MEATS					
Ground beef	20 pound case	45.90	50.97		
Eye rounds	12/6 pounds each	2.42/ pound	3.29/ pound		
Lamb rack	8/2 pounds each	10.50/ pound	15.56/ pound		
Pork chops, bone-in	27/6 ounces each	34.61/case	29.78/ case		
Bacon, 14–18 count	15 pound case	31.98	30.91		
POULTRY					
Chicken breasts, 6 ounce	10 pound case	35.00 (20 #)	18.67		
Turkey cutlets	40/4 ounces each	61.02	—		
Cornish hens	case of 24	43.38 (1/2s)	43.37 (1/2s)		
Diced chicken	10 pound case	29.46	34.40		

CATEGORY	AP UNIT	VENDOR 1 US SUPPLY	VENDOR 2 ZZZ FOODS	VENDOR 3 HOME DAIRY	VENDOR 4 A-1 PRODUCE
SEAFOOD					
Cod fillets, 8 ounce	10 pound case	60.96	72.72		
Shrimp, 16–20 count	20 pound case	149.08	166.66		
Salmon sides	3/2–3 pounds each	11.52/ pound	10.98/ pound		
Imitation crab	24 pound case	33.44 (10#)	76.54		
FRESH PRODUCE					
Yellow onions	50 pound bag	14.66	16.16		
Green onions	2 pound case	5.43	6.00		
Celery	6 count case	14.53	17.54		
Carrots	50 pound bag	34.29	40.00		
Apples	72 count case	50.51	51.88		
DISPOSABLES					
Soufflé cups, 4 ounce	2500/case	49.65	46.50		
Souffle cup lid	2500/case	47.88	44.50		
Plastic wrap, 18-inch	2000 feet	22.75	19.97		
Foil, 18-inch	1000 feet	45.26	38.88		
Punch cups	1000/case	63.68	55.02		

As with US Supply there are a few details that need to be recognized:

- Under "Poultry," ZZZ Foods doesn't offer turkey cutlets at all, so just put a line through it.
- As with the previous supplier, ZZZ Foods only carries the Cornish hens in halves. You may have to change your menu. For now, simply make a notation.

All other prices and pack sizes are correct for ZZZ Foods, so we can move on to the next vendor.

Home Dairy is a company that only supplies dairy products, so you'll only get quotes for a few items on your list. See figure 7.5.

Figure 7.5

CATEGORY	AP UNIT	VENDOR 1 US SUPPLY	VENDOR 2 ZZZ FOODS	VENDOR 3 HOME DAIRY	VENDOR 4 A-1 PRODUCE
DRY INGREDIENTS					
Salt	24/26 ounce	19.58	20.02		
White pepper	18 ounce	19.98	23.10		
Sugar	50 pound bag	48.66	49.20		
All-purpose flour	50 pound bag	18.14	19.00		
Bread crumbs	20 pound case	24.92	25.25		
Raisins	12/2 pound box	59.39 (30#)	52.33		
CANNED GOODS					
Peaches, 35–40 count	6/#10 can	33.74	32.97		
White vinegar	4/1 gallon	13.79	14.87		
Vegetable oil	1 gallon	8.63	9.55		
Honey	5 pound jug	16.51	15.99		
Artichoke hearts	12/14 ounce	—	24.43		
Mayonnaise	4/1 gallon	33.40	36.64		
DAIRY PRODUCTS					
Whole milk	4/1 gallon	16.85	17.05	15.99	
Chocolate milk	4/1 gallon	15.08	16.20	14.99	
Heavy cream	1 quart	6.44 (1/2 gal.)	3.56	6.52 (1/2 gal.)	
Shredded cheddar	5 pound bag	12.61	12.88	11.55	
Large eggs	case/15 dozen	18.27	19.12	18.18	
FROZEN FOOD					
Vanilla ice cream	3 gallon	14.19	17.99	13.99	
Peas	30 pound case	24.68 (20#)	45.00		
French fries	6/5 pound bag	26.03	28.28		
Pie shells	case of 24	31.94	36.78		

Once again, you'll need to make a notation for heavy cream, as Home Dairy only offers it in the half-gallon size. Other than that, all other pack sizes and prices are correct.

Let's move on to the final vendor, A-1 Produce. As with the previous vendor, A-1 Produce will only be able to quote prices for a small portion of your item list, because they only supply produce. The prices are entered in figure 7.6.

Figure 7.6

CATEGORY	AP UNIT	VENDOR 1 US SUPPLY	VENDOR 2 ZZZ FOODS	VENDOR 3 HOME DAIRY	VENDOR 4 A-1 PRODUCE
MEATS					
Ground beef	20 pound case	45.90	50.97		
Eye rounds	12/6 pounds each	2.42/ pound	3.29/ pound		
Lamb rack	8/2 pounds each	10.50/ pound	15.56/ pound		
Pork chops, bone-in	27/6 ounces each	34.61/case	29.78/case		
Bacon, 14–18 count	15 pound case	31.98	30.91		
POULTRY					
Chicken breasts, 6 ounce	10 pound case	35.00 (20 #)	18.67		
Turkey cutlets	40/4 ounces each	61.02	—		
Cornish hens	case of 24	43.38 (1/2s)	43.37 (1/2s)		
Diced chicken	10 pound case	29.46	34.40		
SEAFOOD					
Cod fillets, 8 ounce	10 pound case	60.96	72.72		
Shrimp, 16–20 count	20 pound case	149.08	166.66		
Salmon sides	3/2–3 pounds each	11.52/ pound	10.98/ pound		
Imitation crab	24 pound case	33.44 (10#)	76.54		

CATEGORY	AP UNIT	VENDOR 1 US SUPPLY	VENDOR 2 ZZZ FOODS	VENDOR 3 HOME DAIRY	VENDOR 4 A-1 PRODUCE
FRESH PRODUCE					
Yellow onions	50 pound bag	14.66	16.16		15.00
Green onions	2 pound case	5.43	6.00		5.23
Celery	6 count case	14.53	17.54		14.55
Carrots	50 pound bag	34.29	40.00		34.22
Apples	72 count case	50.51	51.88		50.26
DISPOSABLES					
Soufflé cups, 4 ounce	2500/case	49.65	46.50		
Souffle cup lid	2500/case	47.88	44.50		
Plastic wrap, 18-inch	2000 feet	22.75	19.97		
Foil, 18-inch	1000 feet	45.26	38.88		
Punch cups	1000/case	63.68	55.02		

No other changes are necessary for A-1 Produce, so we can now move on to the comparison stage of costing.

Before any real price comparisons can be made, all items must have apples to apples pricing, meaning that they have the same common denominator—whether it's pack size or weight. Most of our prices already have common denominators, but there are a few that will have to be changed before a meaningful comparison can be made. Observe the following price changes as we enter them on the form.

The raisins price must be changed so that both vendors reflect a per-pound price. The formula is:

Total dollar amount divided by total weight = price per pound

For US Supply, the equation is:

$$\$59.39 \div 30 \text{ pounds} = \$1.979 \text{ per pound}$$

For ZZZ Foods, the formula is $\$52.33 \div 24$ pounds (12/2 pound boxes) = $\$2.18$ per pound. Notice that I always carry out the price three places past the decimal whenever possible, so that I can be sure of the lowest price if it's close between two vendors. It might not mean much if you're only ordering one case of something, but sometimes you might be ordering twenty, thirty, or even one hundred cases of an item and the fractions of a cent per pound will make a difference. We'll enter the new prices next to the original prices on the form as shown in figure 7.7.

Figure 7.7

CATEGORY	AP UNIT	VENDOR 1 US SUPPLY	VENDOR 2 ZZZ FOODS	VENDOR 3 HOME DAIRY	VENDOR 4 A-1 PRODUCE
DRY INGREDIENTS					
Salt	24/26 ounce	19.58	20.02		
White pepper	18 ounce	19.98	23.10		
Sugar	50 pound bag	48.66	49.20		
All-purpose flour	50 pound bag	18.14	19.00		
Bread crumbs	20 pound case	24.92	25.25		
Raisins	12/2 pound box	59.39 (30#)	52.33		
		1.979/ pound	$2.18/ pound		

The price for heavy cream is quoted in two different pack sizes, so let's change the price from ZZZ Foods to a half-gallon price in order to match the other two vendors and add it to the form in figure 7.8. Using your volume measurements, the formula is $3.56 x 2 (2 quarts in a half gallon) = $7.12.

Figure 7.8

DAIRY PRODUCTS					
Whole milk	4/1 gallon	16.85	17.05	15.99	
Chocolate milk	4/1 gallon	15.08	16.20	14.99	
Heavy cream	1 quart	6.44 (1/2 gal.)	3.56 x 2 =$7.12 per ½ gallon	6.52 (1/2 gal.)	
Shredded cheddar	5 pound bag	12.61	12.88	11.55	
Large eggs	case/15 dozen	18.27	19.12	18.18	

The prices for the frozen peas need to be broken down further into a per-pound price for each vendor. The formula for US Supply is $24.68 ÷ 20 pounds = $1.234 per pound, and the formula for ZZZ Foods is $45.00 ÷ 30 pounds = $1.50 per pound. Now we enter them into our table as shown in figure 7.9.

Figure 7.9

FROZEN FOOD					
Vanilla ice cream	3 gallon	14.19	17.99	13.99	
Peas	30 pound case	24.68 (20#) $1.234/pound	45.00 $1.50/ pound		
French fries	6/5 pound bag	26.03	28.28		
Pie shells	case of 24	31.94	36.78		

Next, we'll have to modify the chicken breast prices to get a per-pound price. We use the following formulas and add the prices to the form as shown in figure 7.10. US Supply: $35.00 ÷ 20 pounds = $1.75 per pound. ZZZ Foods: $18.67 ÷ 10 pounds = $1.867 per pound.

Figure 7.10

POULTRY					
Chicken breasts, 6 ounce	10 pound case	35.00 (20 #) $1.75/pound	18.67 $1.867/ pound		
Turkey cutlets	40/4 ounces each	61.02	—		
Cornish hens	case of 24	43.38 (1/2s)	43.37 (1/2s)		
Diced chicken	10 pound case	29.46	34.40		

Finally, the imitation crab will also have to be converted to a per-pound price. Use the following formulas and enter them into the form as shown in figure 7.11. US Supply: $33.44 ÷ 10 pounds = $3.344 per pound. ZZZ Foods: $76.54 ÷ 24 pounds = $3.189 per pound.

Figure 7.11

SEAFOOD					
Cod fillets, 8 ounce	10 pound case	60.96	72.72		
Shrimp, 16–20 count	20 pound case	149.08	166.66		
Salmon sides	3/2–3 pounds each	11.52/ pound	10.98/ pound		
Imitation crab	24 pound case	33.44 (10#) $3.344/ pound	76.54 $3.189/ pound		

Once you've modified all the prices, you can make an apples to apples comparison. Simply compare the prices for each item and highlight the lowest price. You can use check marks, stars, or a marker to highlight the lowest price for each item as shown in figure 7.12.

Figure 7.12

CATEGORY	AP UNIT	VENDOR 1 US SUPPLY	VENDOR 2 ZZZ FOODS	VENDOR 3 HOME DAIRY	VENDOR 4 A-1 PRODUCE
DRY INGREDIENTS					
Salt	24/26 ounce	19.58	20.02		
White pepper	18 ounce	19.98	23.10		
Sugar	50 pound bag	48.66	49.20		
All-purpose flour	50 pound bag	18.14	19.00		
Bread crumbs	20 pound case	24.92	25.25		
Raisins	12/2 pound box	59.39 (30#)	52.33		
		$1.979/ pound	$2.18/ pound		

CATEGORY	AP UNIT	VENDOR 1 US SUPPLY	VENDOR 2 ZZZ FOODS	VENDOR 3 HOME DAIRY	VENDOR 4 A-1 PRODUCE
CANNED GOODS					
Peaches: 35–40 count	6/#10 can	33.74	32.97		
White vinegar	4/1 gallon	13.79	14.87		
Vegetable oil	1 gallon	8.63	9.55		
Honey	5 pound jug	16.51	15.99		
Artichoke hearts	12/14 ounce	—	24.43		
Mayonnaise	4/1 gallon	33.40	36.64		
DAIRY PRODUCTS					
Whole milk	4/1 gallon	16.85	17.05	15.99	
Chocolate milk	4/1 gallon	15.08	16.20	14.99	
Heavy cream	1 quart	6.44 (1/2 gal.)	3.56 x 2 =$7.12 per ½ gallon	6.52 (1/2 gal.)	
Shredded cheddar	5 pound bag	12.61	12.88	11.55	
Large eggs	case/15 dozen	18.27	19.12	18.18	
FROZEN FOOD					
Vanilla ice cream	3 gallon	14.19	17.99	13.99	
Peas	30 pound case	24.68 (20#) $1.234/ pound	45.00 $1.50/ pound		
French fries	6/5 pound bag	26.03	28.28		
Pie shells	case of 24	31.94	36.78		
MEATS					
Ground beef	20 pound case	45.90	50.97		
Eye rounds	12/6 pounds each	2.42/ pound	3.29/ pound		
Lamb rack	8/2 pounds each	10.50/ pound	15.56/ pound		
Pork chops, bone-in	27/6 ounces each	34.61/ case	29.78/ case		
Bacon, 14–18 count	15 pound case	31.98	30.91		

CATEGORY	AP UNIT	VENDOR 1 US SUPPLY	VENDOR 2 ZZZ FOODS	VENDOR 3 HOME DAIRY	VENDOR 4 A-1 PRODUCE
POULTRY					
Chicken breasts, 6 ounce	10 pound case	35.00 (20 #) $1.75/ pound	18.67 $1.867/ pound		
Turkey cutlets	40/4 ounces each	61.02	—		
Cornish hens	case of 24	43.38 (1/2's)	43.37 (1/2's)		
Diced chicken	10 pound case	29.46	34.40		
SEAFOOD					
Cod fillets, 8 ounce	10 pound case	60.96	72.72		
Shrimp, 16–20 count	20 pound case	149.08	166.66		
Salmon sides	3/2–3 pounds each	11.52/ pound	10.98/ pound		
Imitation crab	24 pound case	33.44 (10#) $3.344/ pound	76.54 $3.189/ pound		
FRESH PRODUCE					
Yellow onions	50 pound bag	14.66	16.16		15.00
Green onions	2 pound case	5.43	6.00		5.23
Celery	6 count case	14.53	17.54		14.55
Carrots	50 pound bag	34.29	40.00		34.22
Apples	72 count case	50.51	51.88		50.26
DISPOSABLES					
Soufflé cups, 4 ounce	2500/case	49.65	46.50		
Souffle cup lid	2500/case	47.88	44.50		
Plastic wrap, 18-inch	2000 feet	22.75	19.97		
Foil, 18-inch	1000 feet	45.26	38.88		
Punch cups	1000/case	63.68	55.02		

As you can see, US Supply generally has lower prices. Because of that, they should be your primary vendor and handle most of your supply needs. ZZZ Foods has low enough prices to be your secondary vendor for many items. Home Dairy and A-1 Produce have some low prices and might be used as a supplier some of the time or in an emergency.

What if there's a vendor that you particularly like because they have great service? What if you prefer to use a local company? Well, if they don't have the lowest prices, are you willing to spend more money to use them? I'd say probably not. However, you might be able to get the vendor to match the lowest prices that you've gotten from other companies in order to offer them your business. You could even explain to them that you'd love to buy more products from them, but their prices are too high. Depending on their profit margin or their sales commissions, many companies might be able to work with you. Sometimes even sales associates are willing to take a little off their commission percentages just to get your business. It never hurts to ask.

While we're discussing price changes, I think this is the time to bring up something very important. Just because these vendors have the lowest prices today doesn't mean that they'll always have the lowest prices. In fact, there are some sneaky companies out there who will lowball the competition on pricing initially, just so you'll give them your business when you start out. As time goes on, these tricky rabbits will slowly increase their prices, hoping that you're not paying attention. Many companies don't check their prices regularly. Before you know it, you're paying 25 percent more for the same products that you were buying at great prices eight weeks earlier! Don't allow yourself to be fooled by this tactic!

In order to keep the vendors honest, you're going to have to do price comparisons *every week*. This may seem like a lot of effort, and in some ways it is. However, rich caterers understand that if you're going to run a business that's profitable enough to take you all the way to retirement and beyond, the time that you spend on research will be repaid in dollars. Besides, most large vendors now have websites where you can see the prices for whatever products you want at the touch of a button. You can even print out your own personal order guide of the products you buy every week from each vendor. Then just compare them side by side or write them in your pricing forms.

What if a new vendor comes to town and asks if you want to see its prices? Absolutely! Give the sales representative a copy of your item list and start the process over again, adding the new vendor's prices into the mix. If this new vender has better prices than your current vendors...*great!* At this time, I would caution you against using too many vendors, though. Most need a minimum order amount before they'll even think of delivering to you. Get prices from as many vendors as you want, but only order from your primary and secondary vendors. Otherwise, it really will be complicated to update item prices weekly! You can also add in a specialty supplier or two for emergencies.

Buying in Bulk

As you get more proficient with the food ordering process, you'll notice that some products are much cheaper when you purchase them in larger quantities. A quick glance at a supplier's pack sizes and prices will bear this out.

For instance, if you buy a certain kind of ground beef in a twenty-pound case, you might be able to order that same type of ground beef in an eighty-pound case for a much lower price per pound. Of course you wouldn't want to purchase the bulk ground beef if you couldn't store it for the amount of time necessary to use it up. But if that's not a problem, go for it.

Fresh produce is another area where buying in bulk can be particularly profitable. Let's say that you have been buying yellow onions in a twenty-five-pound case for $13.00. You do a little research and find that there's also a fifty-pound case available for $17.00. If you buy the larger case, you'll receive twice the amount of onions for only $4.00 more. What a deal! As before, you'll have to be able to store the onions and use them up before they start to deteriorate, but if you can do that, this purchase is a no-brainer.

As the owner of your catering business, you're the person who must do the research to find these valuable bulk bargains; no one else is going to do it for you. But, the more you search, the more you're going to find, and the more money you're going to stash away.

Flexibility and the Bottom Line

When you have the basics of food ordering mastered, it's time to add one more profitable wrinkle to the process. That wrinkle is being flexible enough to search out and secure acceptable products that are currently selling at prices well below their normal value. Your ability to use these products will boost your profits toward rich caterer status.

The first thing you have to do is ask your suppliers to put you on the customer list for specials on current or discontinued products. These specials are usually distributed weekly and are snapped up in a hurry by bargain hunters. Although the majority of the products on these lists are usually food items, they can include anything restaurant related. Among the dry ingredients and frozen products, you may find bargains on small-wares for the kitchen or dining room and even office products. You never know what you're going to find! Current items may include overstocked products, items near their expiration dates, or other products not up to specification.

Overstocked products are simply items that were over-ordered by suppliers or overproduced by manufacturers and need to be moved out quickly. When you see something that might fit your catering needs for future events, try to be flexible. Let's say that you normally use three-eighth-inch thick French fries on your menu, but one of your vendors has an abundance of French fries at the five-sixteenth inch size and they're $10.00 cheaper per case. Can you use them? Of course! I doubt that anyone at the event is going to pull out a tape measure and demand a refund. What if you use Red Delicious apples on a regular basis, and, lo and behold, you discover that Golden Delicious apples are on weekly special? I'd say jump on it, reap the savings, and use the cash that you save for something else. What about using a different flavor, such as French vanilla ice cream instead of plain vanilla? How about a different-sized item, like medium eggs instead of large? In the catering business, we use a lot of potatoes. Can you work with random sized potatoes instead of a specific size? Raw chicken breasts can get expensive. Will chicken breast *pieces* work for your menu instead of whole chicken breasts? Every time you peruse a supplier's special pricing sheet, you have an opportunity to pay yourself back. When you add flexibility into your menu, the number of opportunities to save money will seem endless.

Another area where you can save a buck is on products that are nearing their expiration date. This is most important with meat items. Normally a supplier will have a short amount of time to sell a fresh meat item. For our purposes, let's say the item is fresh beef stew meat. When the stew meat is still wholesome, but nearing its sell-by date, it's then put into the freezer by the supplier to sell as frozen stew meat. Depending on the amount of stew meat already in the freezer, the price per case could go down quite a bit. As before, if you have the freezer space and are able to use the product *quickly*, this would be a great buy.

Other meat items work exactly the same way. In our catering business, we use a lot of chicken pieces. Whenever I order chicken for one of our events, I talk to my salesman and ask him for the price of economy chicken. In his company, "economy chicken" is code for chicken that had reached its sell-by date and was frozen. The price for economy chicken is usually quite a bit less than for fresh. When buying this product, my salesman always cautions me to use it within a day or two of thawing, or it might start to deteriorate. This was no problem, since, as I said, we use a lot of chicken. Using this type of product will allow you to serve good quality food at a much lower cost. I suggest that you speak with your suppliers and find out what economy items they may have available. Purchase them when appropriate, and use the savings to make your business more successful.

The next way of spending less on food purchases doesn't happen very often, but when it does, you could receive some big rewards. I'm referring to a product that is produced by one of your suppliers for a specific company according to that company's specifications. For example, let's say that a company known as Winning Wieners does business with one of your suppliers—US Supply. Winning Wieners wants US Supply to produce their quarter-pound hot dogs according to a secret family recipe and not to sell these proprietary hot dogs to anyone but them. The contract is signed, and the hot dogs are produced and shipped to Winning Wieners franchises all over the country. One day, disaster strikes when US Supply realizes that they've made a mistake. A recent batch of Winning Wieners was produced, and each hot dog weighed only three and a half ounces instead of four! What's worse, the supplier didn't discover the mistake until they'd produced and frozen five hundred cases. Yikes! Now what is US Supply going to do? Winning Wieners only wants quarter-pound hot dogs, so they won't accept the smaller size. Since these are specially spiced hot dogs and they weigh less than they're supposed to, they aren't very attractive to many other buyers. The problem is, US Supply has five hundred cases of these bad dogs and must get rid of them as soon as possible.

The next week, your US Supply representative tells you this sad story and mentions that the hot dogs are half price because the warehouse doesn't want to waste their precious space on products that won't sell. So you ask yourself a few questions:

Do I use hot dogs?
Answer: Yes

Do I have storage space?
Answer: Yes

Do I care if the hot dogs are spiced differently?
Answer: No; they're probably even better than the hot dogs I currently buy.

Do I care that they are slightly smaller than I would normally use?
Answer: No, refer back to the French fry/tape measure example.

Do I want to buy something that I use on a regular basis at 50 percent off the regular price?
Answer: You bet!

After thinking about it for about two seconds, you realize this is your chance to scoop up a bargain. You actually hear the cha-ching sound of a cash register bell ringing in your head. With the speed of lightning, you open your mouth and speak the golden words: "I'll order twenty cases." Way to go, baby. You've just made a transaction that would make any rich caterer proud.

This actually happened to me twice: once with hamburger patties (I ordered two hundred cases); and the other with cut-up chicken (I got in late, so there were only ten cases left). Both times

I saved a large amount of money, because I found a way to use odd products, where other caterers couldn't or wouldn't. It was a win-win situation.

All of the previous scenarios stress the importance of flexibility in building your menu and in the way that you structure your food ordering process. Take personal responsibility for searching out money saving opportunities. Buy ingredients in bulk when prices are cheaper and it's appropriate. Have your suppliers and their representatives keep you aware of their weekly pricing specials. Ask your vendors about economy items that may be available to you on a regular basis. And for goodness' sake, ask your suppliers to keep you informed of those bad dog, not-up-to-specification opportunities.

Well done! You have completed your food ordering education. The next part of this bible is geared toward something very controversial that I'm sure you'll have an interest in—leftovers.

THE BOOK OF SUPERABUNDANCE

Part 1: The Leftover Challenge

The Client vs. the Caterer

The Scenario: A client has booked a wedding with you and committed to a guarantee of two hundred guests. On the day of the wedding, for whatever reason, you only serve 150 meals at the reception.

Viewpoint #1: The Client

The bride's father (the client) is visibly disappointed and slightly angry that he'll have to pay for fifty unserved meals. This is understandable, considering the amount of money it's going to cost him. He wants some sort of compensation in the form of a refund or reimbursement. At the very least, he wants to take the leftover food home and use it for another occasion (the next day's gift opening, a family picnic, his upcoming birthday, etc.). It's not your fault, but he wants you to make it right, because he's frustrated.

Viewpoint #2: The Caterer

Of course the caterer has a much different point of view. As always, you have approached this event as one which will exceed the client's expectations and have expended a considerable amount of money to make it so. A sizeable investment in food, labor, and extra-special touches had almost guaranteed a successful event. However, this intensive preparation was based on the profits that you were going to make by serving a guaranteed minimum of two hundred meals. Just because only 150 people showed up doesn't mean that you spent any less money to execute this wonderful wedding reception. As the caterer, you promised to serve food and beverages to all of the guests at this event, and that's what you did. No extra compensation to the client should be necessary. Therefore, the leftover food is yours to do with whatever you wish.

Both the client and the caterer have valid points of view about how this situation should be settled, so a stalemate ensues. Dealing with leftovers is a ticklish issue in the catering industry. Should you give them to the client? Can you keep and reuse them? Should all of them be thrown away? Unfortunately, every caterer does things a little bit differently, which makes the issue even more confusing. In order to resolve this impasse, we'll need to step back and begin at the starting point for this whole issue—the guarantee.

Guaranteed Money

The client guarantees the number of people who plan to attend the event and agrees to pay for those meals. This figure is based primarily on the number of RSVPs the client receives. In our business, we've found that the number of RSVPs a client receives is a relatively accurate predictor of event attendance. Because of this, we encourage our clients to use the RSVP count as the guaranteed number. For the caterer, this guaranteed number translates into the *number of meals* that will be served at the event. You'll keep track of that by counting out the plates before service (at least three times). If the guaranteed number is one hundred people, you should count out one hundred twenty-five plates. You count out 125 because if you run out of plates, you don't want to hurriedly run back to the kitchen and get some more (this leads to miscounting). If the number of meals served is *less* than the guarantee, then the client must pay for the guaranteed number of meals. If the number of meals served is *more* than the guarantee, the client must then pay the guaranteed number plus the number of *additional meals served*. By the way, since all diners are required by state health codes to use a clean plate for each trip to the buffet, each extra trip is another *meal served* and is counted toward the guarantee. Sometimes people who make repeat trips to the buffet actually put you over the guarantee, which is even better for rich caterers!

This guaranteed number is important to you, the caterer, because you'll plan the event around it. Based on this number, you'll decide how much food to order, how many kitchen staff to use, how much equipment to set up, how many servers to hire, etc. If the guaranteed number is considerably higher or lower than the number of meals served, there could be significant problems.

For instance, let's say that the guaranteed number is one hundred people and one hundred and five meals are served. Not to worry—we always prepare enough food for about 5 percent more meals over and above the guarantee and suggest that you do the same. Even if there are no extra people, you can use the additional food to feed all of the event staff who are there working for you. Your employees really appreciate being fed a good meal, and preparing 5 percent more food is just one more way of exceeding the expectations of your clients and staff.

If the guaranteed number is one hundred and the number of meals served is well over that, maybe around one hundred thirty, then you as the caterer might have to go to plan B. Our backup plan is to have an emergency stash of main food items on hand, just in case. This stash includes canned or frozen vegetables, instant mashed potatoes, frozen dinner rolls, etc. We also keep a large pot of simmering water on the stove on the day of the event, to be used for heating those extra vegetables or making the mashed potatoes, should they be needed. Some caterers have an extra pan of the main entrée, or a substitute for it, ready to heat when necessary. If they don't use it, it's frozen and used for the next catered event. If you're going to use a substitute entrée, make the decision a day or two before the event so your staff will know what it is. If you run out of the substitute, you have no choice but to run to the supermarket and buy another entrée that will be acceptable. Hopefully this doesn't happen very often. Sometimes there are fresh foods that can't be replenished quickly because of lack of time or ingredients, such as fresh fruit salad, vegetable trays, pasta salads, etc. In this scenario, we try to stretch these items out as much as possible by using smaller serving utensils or having one of our employees portion them out for the guests. If you run out of these items, don't sweat it. The hot buffet items matter most. Besides, you and the client have agreed that you would prepare and serve enough food for the guaranteed number of people, and then you added on 5 percent as a buffer. After that, if you run out of potato salad or pistachio fluff, so be it.

Now we come to the situation which causes the most friction between caterer and client: the dreaded overinflated guarantee. This means that the client somehow overestimated the guaranteed number, and it turns out to be a much higher number than the actual number of meals served.

When this happens, it's usually the result of something uncontrollable, such as bad weather or a death in the family. Sometimes the client will overestimate because he or she wants to cover all of the bases and make certain there will be enough food for people who probably won't show up. For a large group, the client might add twenty or thirty extra meals to the guarantee number—"just to be sure we don't run out." Or your client may overestimate to take into account invisible guest syndrome. Invisible guests are people who have told the client that they *might* come *if* something else happens. In this case, so-called friends or acquaintances don't want to hurt the host's feelings by telling him or her that they definitely aren't attending the event, so they soften the language a little bit. They'll often say something like, "I might be able to attend if..." and then finish with an implausible situation such as, "My sister doesn't come home that weekend," or "My son's ball game gets cancelled," or the ever popular "If I'm feeling better by then." What they're really saying is: "I'll attend your wedding if I have absolutely nothing else to do!" These people rarely attend, and you should advise your client not to include them in the guaranteed number. As I said before, stick to the actual RSVP number for better accuracy.

The Generous Fool

No matter how the overinflated guarantee situation occurs, the client will probably not be happy about it. You might find that a client-versus-caterer situation develops at the end of the event. It's usually at this point, while your client is as mad as a hornet and maybe even slightly intoxicated, that he or she will get in your face and *demand* the leftovers. In the heat of the moment, it's tempting to simply give the client the leftovers to calm him or her down. However, there's a good chance that your business will suffer as a result of this act of generosity. Eventually, it could transform you from a rich caterer into a generous fool. So, take a deep breath at this point, and try to think logically. Here are some very good reasons why giving leftovers to the client is a bad idea.

1. Sanitation Practices of Ignorant People

If there were no other reason to keep the leftovers from your clients' grasp, this single reason should be enough. There's no one in this universe who will treat your leftover food with as much loving care as you will. When the food that you've prepared is handled or presented poorly by the client, rightly or wrongly, it's a reflection on you and your business. Just imagine giving the excess food to someone in the client's family (who also might be slightly intoxicated), to safeguard until the next time it's heated and served. There are multiple things that can go wrong and turn your fabulous food into a breeding ground for harmful bacteria.

- How long will the food sit in the client's car before being put into a refrigerator?
- Is there enough space in the client's home refrigerator to quickly cool the food to less than forty degrees, or (more likely) will the client stack and mangle the food in order to stuff it in?
- Will the client use clean hands when rearranging cold foods to serve again?
- Will the client reheat the hot food to the proper service temperature in the shortest amount of time?
- Does the client have serving equipment that will hold the hot and cold food at the proper temperatures?
- Will the utensils used to serve the leftover food be clean and sanitary?
- Will the client serve the leftovers outdoors, where excess heat or insects could affect it?
- How long will the food sit out on the client's serving table before being put away?
- Will the client store the leftovers for a second time and use them again?

I've only listed nine areas of concern, but I'm sure you could think of more. What a nightmare!

2. Extra Packaging Expense

If you're still silly enough to consider giving the leftovers to the client after those questions, consider something else. How are you going to hand off the food?

You wouldn't put it in your own containers, because you'll never get them back. You could ask the client for a deposit on the pans, but asking them for more money when they're already upset about paying for invisible people is probably not the best move. Besides, do you really want to deal with that hassle?

The best solution is to put the food in brand-new, clean, disposable containers with lids (that you have to purchase). Now, disposable aluminum or plastic containers are sturdy, but not *that* sturdy. You know that the client is going to stack the pans until at least one of them is crushed. This means that some juicy or gravy laden food is going to leak all over the client's trunk, or even worse, the back seats. Can you say "cleaning bill?" That's what you might be paying if you use such precarious containers. You could refuse to pay the bill, but then the clients will bad-mouth your business all over town. Is it worth it?

No problem, you can double-wrap all of the containers with plastic wrap so that they don't leak. More materials, more labor, more expense, and you'll be paying for all of it. This giving away the leftovers thing is starting to get pricey! Unfortunately, this is just small potatoes compared to what's coming next.

3. **Devastating Financial Liability**

So even after all of my explanations, let's say that you got kicked in the head by a horse, your mind was fuzzy, and you mistakenly gave the clients the leftovers. What if there's a problem and someone gets sick from eating that leftover food? Who do you think the client's going to blame? *You*, that's who! Even though your responsibility should have ended as soon as you gave the food to the client's family, you'll still be blamed for any resulting illness. Who else are they going to blame, themselves? Not a chance. You may even become famous when this disaster becomes a top story on the Internet. Then, not only are the clients and their extended family never going to use your catering service again, the *entire world* will find someone else to cater their events. But that couldn't happen...could it? At the end of this entire fiasco, you've deservedly earned the fate of a generous fool: complete and utter financial ruin.

THE BOOK OF SUPERABUNDANCE

Part 2: Dealing Effectively with Leftovers

Developing Detailed Policies

As a rich caterer, you'll be required to develop a written contract of service. That contract should include a course of action regarding both the guaranteed number and the fate of leftover food. Those policies should be written in such a way that keeps the client happy and also generates the most income for your business.

When developing a policy for your catering contract, make sure that it spells out exactly what's expected from both the client and you. Any hazy or unclear language might come back to bite you later on. This is especially true for something as vitally important as the guaranteed number and leftover food. In our catering business, the contract we submit to the client includes policies concerning both of these key areas. In figure 7.1, you can see the specific language that we use.

Figure 7.1

Guarantee
The guarantee is the minimum number of people for which there will be a charge regardless of the number attending. A guarantee of the number of persons attending your event is required by noon at least ten business days prior to the function date (specify date). (Your catering company) will prepare food for 5 percent more than the guaranteed number. Should there be more meals served at the event than the guarantee, the final charge will be the guaranteed number plus the amount of extra meals served.

Food and Beverage Policy
Food and beverages cannot be brought in by the client for any catered contracted event. This includes milk, coffee, tea, punch, or other alcoholic or nonalcoholic beverages. The only exception to this policy is wedding cake. Also, in observance of state health and safety regulations, the contracting party is not permitted to take home food that's left over from buffets, plated meals, or other catered functions.

After we read these portions of the contract along with the client, we ask if they understand what the guarantee and leftover food policies are saying and how these policies affect them. This is commonly followed by a discussion of what-ifs about how the client should estimate the guaranteed number. We make it clear that the best way to accurately estimate the guaranteed number is to use the RSVP number, and that this has worked very well for our previous clients. We also explain that we prepare enough food for the guaranteed number of guests plus five percent. This should cover the few extra attendees who might show up unexpectedly. In addition, we tell the clients about our backup plan just in case an extra busload of people arrives out of the blue. This is typically enough to assure the client that we'll be handling their event professionally and that they have absolutely nothing to worry about.

As for the leftover food policy, most of the time the client understands the health risks associated with possible mishandling of leftovers by family members. However, that doesn't mean they're happy about it. At this point, we explain that if there's any significant leftover food because of an overestimated guarantee, we'll offer it to their guests at a later time during the event. Normally, this takes the form of a nicely presented snack or sandwich platter later in the evening. That way we can make sure that the leftover food is handled and served properly by our own staff. This is usually enough to satisfy the client, and we move on through the rest of the contract.

You can use our policies word for word if you want (no charge). If you want to invent your own, that's fine too. As we said before, just make sure that your policies are specific and contain all of the information necessary for your particular situation.

Putting Food Back in the Loop

I'm going to tell you a bedtime story, and I want you to put yourself right smack-dab in the middle of it.

You're personally preparing a wonderful meal of roast beef and all the trimmings for a few friends at your home—perhaps a dozen people. Everything goes as planned, and the meal turns out great. Your friends compliment you left and right for the superb job that you did preparing the beef. There is one problem. You were sure that your friends were going to eat more than they did, and now you have a sizable amount of sliced beef and gravy left. No problem, you'll just store the excess dinner in the freezer for another meal. Because you're always a professional, even at home, you handle the leftovers carefully and according to your state sanitation regulations. The food is properly chilled and stored in the freezer. Two months later, you invite the same friends over to watch a football game. The halftime menu includes sliced roast beef sandwiches, using the same beef that you served them before. Halftime arrives, and your hungry friends quickly snatch up the sandwiches. Some of them remark on how great the sliced beef is. When you tell them that the beef is just leftovers from the previous dinner, they remember that meal and remark on how delicious it was. Your friends are also impressed that you took an item as mundane as leftovers and turned it into something really good the second time. There are happy smiles all around. The end.

Were you concerned that your guests were going to get sick? Of course not! You stored and handled the food correctly. Should you feel badly about feeding your friends leftover food? No way; you just gave them a chance to eat your wonderful roast beef a second time. Was this a smart way to save a few nickels while clearing out your freezer? What do you think?

The moral of this story is…well, there is no moral, so forget about that. The point I'm trying to make here is that you can create a delicious meal out of leftover food, if you do it in the right way. In my opinion, there's nothing ethically wrong with doing that.

However, there are some people, even caterers, who'll read this part of the book and be repulsed to the point of scowling. Some may even get angry and curse my name for even *suggesting* this idea. But I know this dirty little secret, and, as a tutor of rich caterers, I'm not afraid to share it with you. So, please sit down and calm yourself before you read the next line. If you're sitting, you may proceed.

A caterer can reuse leftovers and sell them again!

There, I said it, and I'm not ashamed. In fact, many caterers aren't ashamed and use their leftovers as often as they can. I call it putting the food "back in the loop." Other caterers use different terminology, such as "back in the circuit," "into the pipeline," or "recycling." But they all describe using leftover food from one catered event and reselling it at another.

Right now, you're probably thinking of me in one of two ways. Either I'm a greedy catering dog who preys on some future unsuspecting clients for undeserved financial gain, or I'm the smartest son of Albert Einstein. I hope you think the latter. The truth is, if leftovers are handled properly, they can be used to create a quality product in the future and be resold to another client. In fact, using leftovers to positively influence your financial bottom line is so important that...

Properly handling and reusing leftover food is the fifth *nonnegotiable, absolutely essential* part of running a catering business that attracts big money.

Now that you know it's so important, let's get into the nitty-gritty of doing it properly.

Safe Food Handling Is the Key

When working with leftover food, follow these important steps:

Step #1: *Disregard the Food Already Served*

Although rich caterers try as hard as they can to forecast the amount of food necessary for an event, you'll almost always overproduce something. However, not all of the food that's left from an event can be reused. Any food that's left on the buffet is off-limits and should not be put back in the loop. This includes both hot and cold food. The reason for this is twofold. First, the food has been sitting on the buffet table for a while and may have become slightly dried out or its appearance has otherwise deteriorated. This makes it unacceptable for reuse at a future event. Second, the food has been exposed to some time and temperature abuse during service time. Subjecting it to more handling in order to reuse it may cause harmful bacteria to develop. The risk of foodborne illness makes the food unfit for reuse.

So, what can be done with the food left on the buffet line? Well, assuming that the food has been kept at the proper temperatures and is still wholesome to eat, we have three options available.

The first option is to make the food available as a free meal for your event staff. Catering is a labor-intensive business, and your staff needs and deserves a great meal when the guest service is done. They'll also be more willing to work for you again if, in addition to their pay, you provide a wonderful meal. This is a no-brainer: feed the troops.

The second option to consider, after you've fed your staff, is to transform the remaining leftovers into snack or sandwich platters for service later on in the event. Get the client's permission first (they always say yes), and then dazzle them a second time. Condense and redesign any cold platters (hors d' oeuvres, cheese, vegetables and dip, etc.), and add fresh garnishes so that they look full and beautiful again before service. Make small sandwiches out of any leftover sliced meats and remaining dinner rolls (if the meat is still hot, chill it first), and pile the sandwiches high on a decorated platter. Be creative and have fun with this, knowing that you're about to exceed the client's expectations once again. Keep the trays cold until you're ready to serve them. When the client gives you the okay to start the second service, bring the platters out with a flourish, and put them where most of the guests are congregating (usually around the bar). Most people are hungry again toward the end of the evening, and the food will disappear in a hurry. At this point, you're pretty certain that the client is very happy with your work and will spread the word to friends and acquaintances. Happy clients and more business—what a great way to use leftovers!

The third option, unfortunately, is to toss all that remains after the first two options into the scrap heap. Rich caterers hate to throw food away and sometimes weep when it happens. They know that even unusable leftovers have a value, and it hurts their business to throw them away. To them (and hopefully to you), it's like tossing dollar bills into the dumpster. But don't be too upset; a small amount of waste is to be expected at any large event. As long as you've kept the waste to a minimum, you and your staff have done the best job possible.

Step #2: *Evaluate the Food Quality*

If the client ends up overinflating the guaranteed number, then the amount of leftovers back in the kitchen could increase dramatically. This is the food that we'll be trying our best to salvage. Right after your staff serves the guests, make a thorough inspection of all the leftover food.

For the hot food, make your inspection as soon as it comes out of the oven or warming cabinet. When hot foods have been held at serving temperatures for a while, there's usually at least a slight deterioration in food quality. On the flip side, cold food is normally stored safely in the refrigerator, so there really should be no alteration in quality. Inspect cold food after you've finished inspecting the hot food. As you inspect both hot and cold leftovers, there are a few questions you should be asking yourself about the quality of the food:

1. Has the extended holding time changed the food's color, flavor or texture?
   Example: You cooked fresh, beautiful green beans for an event. After sitting in the warmer for three hours, the leftover beans taste fine, but the texture is softer, and the color is a dull olive green. This will lead you to question number two.

2. Can the food be restored (or nearly) to its original quality and served as is?
   Example: The leftover food that you're inspecting is sliced turkey and gravy. You'll have to decide whether you can serve it again as sliced turkey and gravy or not. If the food can't be served as is, move on to question number three.

3. Can the food be used as an ingredient in a different recipe?
   Example: Can the green beans be used to make another item on your menu, like green bean casserole? Can the turkey be added to turkey soup? In other words, is it worth the time and effort to save the leftovers and use them in something else? The answer to this is usually yes. It may not make sense to save an item like chicken wings, where the effort to remove the bones and skin wouldn't yield enough meat to make it worthwhile. With a situation like that, you can either give the wings to the staff (to eat before they go home) or take them home and eat them yourself.

Step #3: *Treat the Leftover Food with Extra Care*

If the leftover items you've chosen to keep are handled using proper sanitation practices, there's no reason in the world why they couldn't be reused and resold to future clients. In fact, we'd be foolish if we didn't reuse leftovers in this way, because it makes our business more profitable. Below are some guidelines for handling leftovers that are going to be put back in the loop.

Hot Leftovers

1. Chill or freeze hot foods promptly after inspection. A hot liquid, such as soup or gravy, will cool faster if it's put into a clean metal pot or bain-marie and placed in ice water. Stir the food occasionally while chilling to distribute the temperature better and cool it faster.

2. Large amounts of more solid items should be divided into smaller portions and placed in shallow containers for quicker chilling. Make sure that the refrigerator is large enough *and* cold enough to handle the amount of hot leftovers you place there. The cooler should be able to hold a steady temperature of forty degrees Fahrenheit or below, even with the hot food inside it.

3. Don't cover the food too tightly in the refrigerator, because it will hold the heat in. Use a loosely fitting lid, or cover the pans lightly with plastic wrap, and leave a corner uncovered. This will allow steam to escape.

4. Take periodic temperature readings to make sure that the food being chilled is under seventy degrees Fahrenheit after two hours and under forty degrees Fahrenheit after four hours. If a leftover item is to be frozen, make sure that the food is completely chilled before putting it in the freezer.

5. Before putting the chilled food in its final resting place (cooler or freezer), make sure to tightly cover, label, and date the containers. Food items to be frozen should be wrapped completely and securely in plastic wrap. I usually wrap the entire pan twice, once in each direction. By doing this, I know that the wrap won't fly off and cause freezer burn before I can use the food. In addition, the extra plastic wrap allows me to stack a few pans on top of each other after they're frozen without worrying about the seal breaking.

6. Reheat any leftovers to be served as is, up to 165 degrees Fahrenheit throughout. Reheat sauces, soups, and gravies to a rolling boil for one minute.

Cold Leftovers

1. Evaluate whether the cold item can be kept in the same serving bowl or tray for service the next day. If so, make sure that it's covered tightly, labeled, and dated. Then place it in the refrigerator where it won't be disturbed before service time.
2. If the item needs to be stored in a different container, remove the food to a clean storage container(s) and cover, label, and date it.

For both hot and cold leftovers, be sure to use them up as quickly as possible in order to retain their good quality.

Creatively Transforming Leftover Food

Here are a few ways that we put leftovers back in the loop. You're more than welcome to use any of these ideas to help you become a rich caterer:

Leftover cooked vegetables: Mix leftover cooked vegetables with a seasoned sauce to make a tasty vegetable casserole. I've already mentioned the green bean casserole, which uses mushroom soup. You can also blend the vegetables with an herbed white sauce, cheese sauce, or Alfredo sauce to make things interesting. Try mixing the sauce with more than one type of vegetable for a little variety. Broccoli and cauliflower or peas and carrots are examples of vegetables that pair well together. Sprinkle the top with some buttered bread crumbs, crushed-up croutons, or chopped-up onion rings—all made from leftovers. Bake the casserole until the topping is golden brown and serve. Your client will rave about how delicious it is and ask for the recipe!

Leftover potatoes: Leftover cooked potatoes can be transformed into an array of secondary dishes. With the addition of some milk, butter, and seasonings, boiled or steamed potatoes are great for making mashed potatoes. Baked potatoes can be peeled and cubed and then used for au gratin potatoes, potato salad, or clam chowder. Save the peelings if you want and use them later for loaded potato skins. Fried potatoes can be made into hash browns, added to stews, or chopped into tiny pieces and used to top tuna casserole (think potato chips). I bet if you thought really hard, you could come up with at least twenty more ideas.

Leftover meats: Meats that have been in the warmer for any length of time tend to dry out, so the conversion process will usually involve a sauce. Leftover sliced meats (beef, pork, turkey) can be reheated with gravy and used to build meat and gravy sandwiches. Add barbecue sauce and spices to cooked, shredded meat, and it turns into filling for BBQ sandwiches. Use that same shredded meat, add Mexican spices, and it's magically converted into taco or enchilada filling. My personal favorite is to take leftover cooked turkey, mix it with leftover stuffing and leftover gravy (really, I'm not kidding), heat it up, and serve it on buns as a turkey and dressing sandwich. It's delicious and inexpensive. I haven't seen anyone yet who hasn't *loved* them!

Leftover cheese: Cheese spread that's been formed into balls, logs, pyramids, or whatever and wrapped tightly can be stored securely in the refrigerator or freezer and used again as is. Untouched sliced or cubed cheese trays can be used again as is as long as they've been sealed securely. Any other leftover cheese that has not been served can be shredded and used for cheese sauce or casserole toppings.

Leftover fruit: Fresh fruit doesn't last very long, so leftover options are a little more limited. As with cheese, untouched fresh fruit bowls or trays can be used again as long as they've been sealed securely. I wouldn't wait much past twenty-four hours to serve them, though. Some fruit can be frozen and later baked into coffee cakes or muffins. If you're really talented, extra fruit can be cooked, thickened, and made into fruit fillings for pies or fruit toppings for cheesecakes. Another good way to use leftover frozen fruit is to thaw it out and drain the juice. We use that delicious fresh fruit juice as an ingredient for our wedding punch. You can also mix the fruit juice with red wine and a touch of brandy to turn it into the most *incredible* sangria.

Those are just a few ideas to help you put your leftovers back in the loop. There are plenty more in other books and on the Internet. Never stop creating new and interesting recipes using leftovers, and offer them to your clients as specials whenever possible. When you run out of leftover creations, go back to your regular menu and start all over again. Using your leftovers creatively, effectively, and profitably is what it's all about for rich caterers like you.

In Conclusion...

In this volume, I've tried my best to offer you the most important information to help you generate extra income through the proper handling of the food you purchase and serve. There's always more, of course, and I recommend that you continue your research even after you become a rich caterer. Now I hope you'll move on to the second volume of this rich caterer duo entitled, *The Testament of Service* and become an even *richer* caterer.

This is (literally) the bottom line:

"Watch the pennies and the
dollars take care of themselves."

—*Mr. Perlowitz*

APPENDIX 1
Yield Percentages of Common Fruits and Vegetables

The percentages listed are close approximates to be used for yield calculations. Actual yields for the following items will be slightly higher or lower based on their condition and the amount and type of trimming done for each fruit or vegetable.

Item	% Yield	Item	% Yield
Artichokes: globe	80%	Apples: all varieties	75%
Beans: green or wax	87%	Avocados	75%
Beets: tops off	75%	Bananas	70%
Broccoli: full with stalk	70%	Berries: all varieties	93%
Brussels sprouts	80%	Grapefruit: sections only	47%
Cabbage: green,		Kiwi fruit: peeled	80%
white, or red	80%	Lemon/limes: juiced	43%
Carrots	78%	Mangoes	75%
Cauliflower	55%	Melons: all varieties	50%
Celery	75%	Oranges: sections only	62%
Corn on the cob	27%	Papayas	65%
Cucumbers	85%	Peaches: pitted and	
Eggplant: peeled	75%	peeled	75%
Garlic	87%	Pears	75%
Iceberg lettuce	75%	Pineapple	50%
Mushrooms: uncooked	90%	Plums: pitted only	95%
Onions	90%	Rhubarb	87%
Parsley	85%		
Peas: edible pod	90%		
Bell peppers: all colors	82%		
Potatoes: white or sweet	80%		
Spinach/other greens	60%		
Squash: summer	90%		
Squash: winter	75%		
Tomatoes: peeled	90%		
Turnips/rutabagas	77%		

APPENDIX 2

Sample Menus - The following are examples of our menu items.

Rich Catering
Buffet Choices

Traditional Fare: (least expensive—insert price) per person

Entrée Selections (choose two)

Beef
Roast Beef with Gravy
Swiss Steak
Homemade Meatloaf
Salisbury Steak
Braised Beef Tips with Gravy
Meatballs (BBQ or Marinara)

Pork
Baked Ham
Ham Loaf
Roast Pork with Gravy
BBQ Pork

Poultry
Baked Chicken
BBQ Chicken
Roast Turkey with Gravy

Seafood
Baked Whitefish with Lemon
    Butter

Vegetarian
Spaghetti with Marinara Sauce
Vegetable Lasagna
Macaroni and Cheese

Casseroles
Beef Stew
Spaghetti with Meat Sauce
Meat Lasagna
Tuna Casserole
Chicken ala King
Scalloped Potatoes with Ham
Layered Shredded Pork
    Enchiladas

Salad Selections (choose two)

Tossed Green Salad
Coleslaw
Vegetable Pasta
Macaroni Salad

Mayonnaise Potato Salad
Cottage Cheese
Jello

Starch Selections (choose two)

Macaroni and Cheese
Buttered Herb Pasta
Rice Pilaf
Scalloped Potatoes

Baked Potatoes
Mashed Potatoes
Oven Roasted Potatoes
Sage Stuffing

Vegetable Selections (choose two)

Baked Beans
Seasoned:
  • Green Beans
  • Corn

  • Peas
  • Carrots
  • Beets

Bread and Roll Selections (choose one)

Buttermilk Biscuits
Baking Powder Biscuits
Assorted Dinner Rolls
Hard Rolls

Bread Sticks
French Bread
White Bread
Wheat Bread

Beverage Selections

Coffee (decaf and regular)   Water

Any substitutions from the Premium Menu will be $1.00 additional per person for each substitution.
Any substitutions from the Elegant Menu will be $2.00 additional per person for each substitution.

Rich Catering
Buffet Choices

Premium Menu: (more expensive—insert price) per person

Entrée Selections (choose two)

Beef
Braised Stuffed Beef Roll-Ups
Braised or BBQ Beef Short Ribs
Beef Stroganoff
Country Fried Steak
Teriyaki Steak
Swedish Meatballs

Pork
Pork Chops with
    Mushroom Gravy
Breaded Pork Cutlets
BBQ Pork Spareribs
Sweet and Sour Pork
Italian Sausage
Bratwurst
Glazed Ham (carved)

Poultry
Stuffed Chicken Breast
Grilled Herb Chicken Breast
Italian Baked Chicken
Chicken Parmesan
Teriyaki Chicken
Sweet and Sour Chicken
Baked Herb Chicken Breast
Roast Turkey Breast (carved)

Seafood
Italian Baked Fish
Baked Salmon Almandine
Jambalaya

Vegetarian
Stuffed Shells Marinara
Bean and Cheese Enchiladas

Casseroles
Pepper Steak
Hungarian Goulash
Chicken Chow Mein
Chicken and Dumplings
Turkey Tetrazzini
Turkey Potpie
Chicken Potpie
Pasta Primavera (ham and
    vegetables)
Stuffed Shells Marinara
Stuffed Peppers
Cabbage Rolls
Au Gratin Potatoes with Ham

Mexican
Tacos (beef or chicken)
Fajitas (beef or chicken)
Enchiladas (beef or chicken)

Salad Selections (choose two)

Deluxe Green Salad
Oriental Coleslaw
Cucumber and Onions with
  Sour Cream
Carrot and Raisin Salad
Hot Bacon Potato Salad

Italian Potato Salad
Triple Bean Salad
Mixed Vegetable Salad
Taco Salad
Perfection Salad
Ambrosia Fruit Salad

Starch Selections (choose two)

Herbed Rotini
Noodles Romanoff
Vegetable Rice Pilaf
Vegetable Fried Rice
Spanish Rice
Potato Skins
Hash Browns

Garlic Mashed Potatoes
Parsley Buttered Potatoes
Au Gratin Potatoes
O'Brien Potatoes
Lyonnaise Potatoes
Glazed Sweet Potatoes
Buttered Baby Red Potatoes

Vegetable Selections (choose two)

Broccoli or Cauliflower
  (Almandine, Cheese Sauce,
  or Lemon Butter)
Green Beans Almandine
Green Beans w/ Mushrooms
Green Bean Casserole
Calico Baked Beans
Refried Beans

Corn O'Brien
Herbed Summer Squash
Glazed Carrots
Peas with Mushrooms
Creamed Peas with Pearl
  Onions
Herbed Vegetable Medley
Mixed Vegetable Stir-Fry

Bread and Roll Selections (choose two)

Fruit Muffins
Cracked Wheat Rolls
Marble Rye Rolls

Garlic Bread
Garlic Bread Sticks
Sourdough Rolls

Beverage Selections (all available)

Coffee (regular and decaf)   Water   Iced Tea

Any substitutions from the Elegant Menu will be $2.00 additional per person for each substitution.

Rich Catering
Buffet Choices

Elegant Menu: (most expensive—insert price) per person

Entrée Selections (choose two)

Beef
Beef Kabobs
Burgundy Beef
Stuffed Flank Steak (carved)
Smoked Beef Brisket (carved)
Prime Rib (carved)
Curried Beef

Pork
Roast Pork Loin (carved)
Smoked Pork Loin (carved)
BBQ Pork Back Ribs
Pork New Orleans
Pork Kabobs
Smoked Polish Sausage
Curried Pork

Seafood
Southern-Style Crab Cakes
Creole Shrimp
Seafood Au Gratin
Seafood Newburg
Salmon Kabobs
Baked Fish Steaks (tuna,
   swordfish, halibut)
Shrimp Stir-Fry
Curried Seafood

Poultry
Chicken Cordon Bleu
Chicken with Mushroom and
   Wine Sauce
Roast Cornish Hen
Chicken Breast Cacciatore
Grilled Chicken Dijon
Chicken Crepes
Chicken Kabobs
Smoked Chicken
Turkey Kabobs
Smoked Turkey (carved)
Curried Turkey
Curried Chicken

Vegetarian
Tortellini Marinara
Vegetable Stir-Fry
Fettuccini Alfredo
Vegetable Alfredo

Casseroles
Stir-Fry (any meat)
Beef Potpie
Chicken Divan
Chicken Pasta Alfredo
Shrimp Pasta Alfredo

Salad Selections (choose two)

Mesclun Salad (baby greens)
Broccoli and Bacon Salad
Caramel Apple Salad
Marinated Mushrooms
Spaghetti Parmesan Salad

Waldorf Salad
Fresh Fruit Salad
Meat Pasta Salad
Seafood Pasta Salad

Starch Selections (choose two)

Tortellini Marinara
German Spaetzle
Fettuccini Alfredo
Red Beans and Rice
Curried Rice Pilaf
Italian Risotto
Cheesy Mashed Potatoes
Twice Baked Potatoes

Duchess Potatoes
Sour Cream Potatoes
Mashed Garlic Red Potatoes
Mashed Potatoes with Cheese
   and Bacon
Potato Pancakes
Vegetable Couscous

Vegetable Selections (choose two)

Asparagus with Lemon Butter
Asparagus with Cheese Sauce
Ranch-Style Red Beans
Black Beans
Eggplant Parmesan
Herbed Spaghetti Squash

Mini Corn on the Cob
Ratatouille Vegetable
   Casserole
Onion and Swiss Cheese Bake
Brandied Mushroom
   Casserole

Bread and Roll Selections (choose two)

Mini Croissants
Onion Butterflake Rolls
Bread Loaves or Rolls:
- Tomato Dill Bread
- Multigrain Bread

- Cracked Wheat Bread
- Pumpernickel Bread
- Marble Rye Bread
- Challah (egg) Bread

Beverage Selections (all available)

Coffee
Water
Lemonade

Iced Tea
Hot Flavored Teas

Rich Catering
Sandwich Buffet Choices

Traditional Fare: (least expensive—insert price) per person

Bread Selections

Buttermilk Biscuits
Assorted Dinner Rolls
Hamburger Buns
Hot Dog Buns
Hard Rolls
White Bread
Whole Wheat Bread

Cold Selections

Pork
Ham Salad
Roast Pork
Honey Ham

Poultry
Chicken Salad
Turkey Salad
Roast Turkey

Vegetarian
Egg Salad
Three Cheese
Mixed Vegetable

Hot Selections

Beef
Sloppy Joe
Hamburger

Pork
Honey Ham
Pulled Pork
Roast Pork and
    Dressing
Braised Pork and
    Gravy
Hot Dog

Poultry
Roast Turkey with
    Gravy
Roast Turkey with
    Dressing
Sliced Turkey
Chicken and
    Dressing

172

Condiments

Butter

Mayonnaise

Yellow Mustard

Brown Mustard

Pickles/Relish

Ketchup

Accompaniment Selections

Salads

Tossed Green Salad

Macaroni Salad

Vegetable Pasta

Coleslaw

Mayonnaise Potato Salad

Cottage Cheese

Jello

Side Dishes

Macaroni and Cheese

Buttered Herb Pasta

Scalloped Potatoes

Baked Potatoes

Mashed Potatoes

Oven Roasted Potatoes

Potato Chips

Baked Beans

Seasoned:

- Green Beans
- Corn
- Peas
- Carrots
- Beets

This menu includes a choice of two meats (cold or hot), two breads, three accompaniments (salads or side dishes), and all condiments. Coffee and ice water are also included. Any substitutions from the Premium Menu will be a $.50 additional charge per person for each substitution. Any substitutions from the Elegant Menu will be a $1.00 additional charge per person for each substitution. American or Swiss cheese is available for an additional charge of $.40 per person.

Rich Catering
Sandwich Buffet Choices

Premium Fare: (more expensive—insert price) per person

Bread Selections

All Traditional Selections
available plus:
Bread Loaves or Rolls:
- Cracked Wheat

- Marble Rye
- Sourdough
- Brat Buns

Cold Selections

Beef
Roast Beef
Meatloaf

Pork
Salami

Vegetarian
Tuna Salad
Tuna and Egg
Salad

Hot Selections

Beef
Meatloaf with Gravy
Meatball
Sliced Roast Beef
Shredded BBQ
Beef
Hamburger
(quarter pound)
Mexican Shredded
Beef

Pork
Bratwurst
Shredded BBQ
Pork
Smoked Polish
Sausage
Italian Sausage
Mexican Shredded
Pork
Cheddarwurst

Poultry
BBQ Chicken
BBQ Turkey
Mexican Shredded
Chicken
Mexican Shredded
Turkey
Grilled Chicken
Breast

Condiments

All Traditional
Selections
available plus:

Horseradish Sauce
Honey Mustard
Dijon Mustard

Cranberry Salsa
Ranch Dressing
Garlic Mayonnaise

Accompaniment Selections

All Traditional Selections available plus:

Salads

Deluxe Green
    Salad
Asian Coleslaw
Carrot and Raisin
    Salad

Hot Bacon Potato
    Salad
Italian Potato Salad
Triple Bean Salad
Mixed Vegetable
    Salad

Taco Salad
Perfection Salad
Ambrosia Fruit
    Salad

Side Selections

Herbed Rotini
Noodles Romanoff
Vegetable Rice Pilaf
Spanish Rice
Potato Skins
Hash Browns
Garlic Mashed
    Potatoes
Parsley Buttered
    Potatoes
Au Gratin Potatoes
O'Brien Potatoes

Glazed Sweet
    Potatoes
Broccoli (Lemon
    Butter or Cheese
    Sauce)
Green Beans
    Almandine
Green Beans with
    Mushrooms
Green Bean
    Casserole
Calico Baked Beans

Corn O'Brien
Herbed Summer
    Squash
Glazed Carrots
Peas with
    Mushrooms
Creamed Peas with
    Onions
Herbed Vegetable
    Medley
Mixed Vegetable
    Stir-Fry

This menu includes a choice of two meats (cold or hot), two breads, three accompaniments (salads or side dishes), and choice of condiments. Coffee, iced tea, and water are included. Any substitutions from the Elegant Menu will be a $1.00 additional charge per person for each substitution. American or Swiss cheese is available for an additional charge of $.40 cents per person.

Rich Catering
Sandwich Buffet Choices

Elegant Fare: (most expensive—insert price) per person

Bread Selections

All Traditional and Premium Selections available plus:
Bread Loaves or Rolls:
- Tomato Dill
- Multigrain
- Cheese
- Pumpernickel
- Onion Rye
- Marble Onion Rye
- Challah (egg) Bread

Cold Selections

Beef
Italian Beef
Pastrami
Corned Beef

Poultry
Smoked Turkey

Combination
Club (Roast Beef,
    Ham, Turkey)
Italian (Pastrami,
    Pepperoni,
    Salami)

Hot Selections

Beef
Italian Beef
Pastrami
Corned Beef
Philly Steak

Poultry
Smoked Turkey
Chicken Breast
    (choice of style)
- Teriyaki
- Southwestern
- Tuscan
- Bourbon

Seafood
Baked Salmon
Grilled Tuna
Tilapia Reuben

Vegetarian
Portabella
    Mushroom
Fresh Mozzarella
    and Tomato

Condiments

All Traditional
  Selections
  available plus:
Lemon Tarragon
Creamy Parmesan
  Peppercorn

Raspberry Vinaigrette
Guacamole
Creamy Basil Pesto
Smoky Chipotle

Red Wine
  Vinaigrette

Accompaniment Selections

All Traditional Selections available plus:

Salads

Mesclun Salad
  (baby greens)
Broccoli and Bacon
  Salad
Marinated
  Mushrooms

Spaghetti Parmesan
  Salad
Waldorf Salad
Fresh Fruit Salad
Meat Pasta Salad

Cucumber and
  Onions with Sour
  Cream
Seafood Pasta Salad

Side Selections

Tortellini Marinara
German Spaetzle
Fettuccini Alfredo
Any Meat Fried
    Rice
Red Beans and Rice
Curried Rice Pilaf
Italian Risotto
Cheesy Mashed
    Potatoes
Red Skinned
    Mashed Potatoes
Twice Baked
    Potatoes
Duchess Potatoes
Sour Cream
    Potatoes

Mashed Garlic Red
    Potatoes
Mashed Potatoes
    with Cheese and
    Bacon
Potato Pancakes
Sweet Potato
    Soufflé
Vegetable Couscous
Jamaican Rice and
    Peas
Asparagus with
    Lemon Butter
Asparagus with
    Cheese Sauce
Ranch-Style Red
    Beans

Black Beans
Eggplant Parmesan
Herbed Spaghetti
    Squash
Mini Corn on the
    Cob
Ratatouille
Vegetable
    Casserole
Onion and Swiss
    Cheese Bake
Brandied
    Mushroom
    Casserole
Fried Green
    Tomatoes

This menu includes a choice of two meats (cold or hot), two breads, three accompaniments (salads or side dishes), and choice of condiments. Coffee, iced tea, hot flavored teas, lemonade, and ice water are included. American or Swiss cheese is available for an additional charge of $.40 cents per person.

20384067R00100

Made in the USA
Charleston, SC
09 July 2013